REAL WOMEN OF THE REGENCY

*Romance, Affairs, Fashion, Authors to Actresses
& Women Leaders*

LEAH GAIL

Cover Design: dezinir.99

ISBN: 9798354517008 (Paperback)

ABOUT THE AUTHOR

Leah is an author and history lover living in the beautiful Cotswolds, in the heart of Shakespeare country in the UK.

Leah's background is in Music Marketing. Having worked in an industry with very few women at the top, she spends the majority of her time mentoring her peers to assist them in their careers. Leah has also been enlisted into the Women in Music Roll of Honour, which recognises game changers within the industry who have helped other women to reach their potential.

Leah's first book, '**Extraordinary Women in History**' encourages readers to dream big and not allow barriers to get in their way. She hopes that her books will inspire and empower other women.

'**Real Women of the Regency**", Leah's second book, looks back at the real lives of women during the Regency era. These are women of all backgrounds who each became influential, powerful figures in their own right. They are the influencers of their own day.

To keep up to date on other books, you can follow Leah on Instagram and Facebook:

 @leahgailauthor

 @leahgailauthor

For further information, please sign up to the mailing list here: leahgail.com

BOOKS AVAILABLE

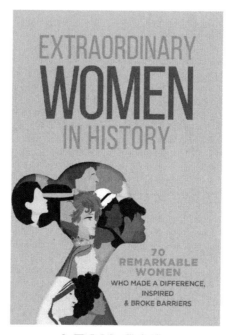

Point your phone camera at the QR codes to purchase on Amazon.

CONTENTS

Introduction – A Right Royal Crisis 1

Chapter 1 – Crippling Conventions: The Rules of Romance 13

Chapter 2 – An Eye for Style and Elegance: Regency Fashion 35

Chapter 3 – Behind the Scenes: The Work of Political Hostesses 47

Chapter 4 – From Austen to Shelley: The Regency's Female Authors 61

Chapter 5 – All the World's a Stage: Actresses and Artistes 91

Chapter 6 – Making a Difference 107

Chapter 7 – Casting off the Chains: Black Women of the Regency 135

Chapter 8 – Lesbians, Cross Dressers and Other Taboos 157

Chapter 9 – Behind Closed Doors: Not So Secret Affairs 173

Conclusion – Legacies of the Regency 205

References 209

INTRODUCTION

A RIGHT ROYAL CRISIS

Imagine a time when keeping up with the social Joneses is of such importance that a rotting pineapple forms the centrepiece of a posh society dinner. Not at a meal for the highest strata of society, admittedly. The pungent pineapple was a fine spiky specimen when it graced that occasion. The fruit is passed down through levels of social niceties, at each stage looking a little less appetising and a little more bruised until it reaches its present home.

Despite its broken leaves and leaking, fizzing juices, the pineapple is still much admired. It will be because this is the Regency period, and appearances are all. Never mind that all is mushy and corrupted inside the skin of the golden ananas. It's a pineapple, and therefore it must be good. Just don't look too closely.

If we are to pick a maxim for Regency times, that will be it. Don't look too closely. Because if we do, we might see things we'd rather pretend are not there.

This is an era where the club-footed poet, Lord Byron, could advocate free love and then demonstrate his commitment to the ideal by luring as many women as he could manage to his bed. Where a cobbler's daughter from Devon could pass muster as a mysterious South Sea Islands Princess, provided she adopts an accent and bastardises the odd foreign-sounding word. Or a real Princess, Sophia, could have an illegitimate son (whose father might even be the Princess's own brother) who is abandoned to an ordinary life in Weymouth rather than allow society to become aware of a Royal's promiscuity.[1]

The Regency is a time of contradiction; abolitionists fought tooth and nail for the freedom of slaves while a woman was burned at the stake for counterfeiting some coins. When conventions require the wearing of a virtual ironing board to keep one's back straight, lest a young lady be thought to be slouching but will turn a blind eye if the same woman embarks on an affair with a married man even if she is married herself. In fact, that kind of infidelity is regarded as more acceptable than a young single woman asking a man to dance or laughing out loud at a joke.

It is a time when the rich wear the finest linens and most beautifully designed clothes, whilst the future king's wife can go for months without bathing. Yet the only thing stronger than her body odour is the popularity she enjoys among the people.

We enjoy the Regency in so many forms. From the glorious landscape paintings that emerged from the times to the stunning architecture found in towns such as Brighton, Bath and Cheltenham. We adore the novels of Austen, and TV stations abound with adaptations of her works. A programme such as the Netflix Drama 'Bridgerton' can trance a nation with its glorious costumes, evocative settings and sexual impropriety. But what is the Regency? And crucially, how did it come about?

Nearly two hundred and fifty years have passed since George III's adored sons, Prince Alfred and Prince Octavius, died just eight months apart. Alfred was not quite two, and Octavius was just four years old. Each was a king's favourite, especially little Octavius. George is a complex man, harsh on himself and his children. He adores his daughters but restricts their freedom. He falls out with his sons, and they escape his control as soon as possible. Not the youngest ones, though. These junior members of his family are indulged and adored.

But threats to the well-being of young children come in many forms. One of the most dangerous is smallpox.

There is a vaccination of sorts for the disease, but it is risky. It involves infecting a healthy child with a tiny dose of the virus and trusting that their young bodies can cope with this low-level infection. If so, they will fight it off and develop the immunity which will stay with them throughout their lives. Most of the inoculated recover from their jab quickly. But in about three per cent of cases, the infection takes hold and becomes life-threatening. For many of these victims, death follows.

That is what happens to Alfred, already a sickly child, in the summer of 1782. Only eight months later, George's beloved Octavius succumbs in exactly the same way. George III has no less than fifteen children. Nothing, though, makes the loss of these two any easier. He enters a period of depression, guilt and mourning.

When George was around fifteen, he suffered from some kind of malaise. The problem is hidden away; nobody wants their future king to be afflicted with a disturbing condition. Whatever the problem might be, it passes, and a few years later, George is crowned king. He is in his early forties when first Alfred and then Octavius die. George is heartbroken. He dreams of the children, believing they are coming to him and speaking to him. He carries a pillow around, hugging it and talking to it as though it is Octavius. He commissions a painting to be hung above his bed, the first thing he witnesses on waking in the morning. In the painting, Alfred waits in heaven, welcoming Octavius as his older brother joins him.

By 1788 George's mental state is in disarray. He suffers another bout of severe depression, mixed with moments of intense mania. His doctors purge him, blister him, lock him away. He is placed in a straitjacket – a procedure at the time considered kind – an enforced hug of yourself. Members of the new breed of doctor – psychologists - are brought in. This is a time when the dreaded hospital of Bedlam treated the mentally ill by chaining them up. Treatment is crude in the extreme and almost certainly causes more harm than good. Parliament, urged on by the opportunist Prince of Wales, considers that they may need to create a Regency. In fact, George III himself, during one of his many bouts of self-doubt, had advised as such some years before.

Then the mania passes. George regains his equilibrium. The danger fades at first but then returns again and again, each time more seriously than before. Parliament is slow to act, maybe because the Regency will promote the Prince of Wales, and he is a repulsive waster, a drunk and a serial womaniser. But this is a time of global unrest. In America, Independence has been claimed. Closer to home, an assassination attempt is made on the king. Most alarmingly of all, across the English Channel, the French Royal family will soon be overthrown and executed. No person holding any kind of power wishes to make insurrection a more likely outcome than it already is. Appointing a deeply unpopular person such as the Prince of Wales as head of state does make revolution more likely, and that will have implications for every person of status and wealth. The Regency Act is put on ice, and Parliament prays that George III will recover. Then, in 1810, another young child of George died, his adored Princess Amelia. He plunged once again into a period of madness. The Regency bill was passed in February 1811. It remains in existence until the king dies, unstable, deranged and senile, in 1820.

For this reason, the Regency officially runs from 1811 until 1820. However, because of the King's illness, the era is taken as being from 1790, when the old king's mental health was first publicly noted as being in decline, until the death of the Prince of Wales, later George IV, in 1830.

This is not a book about George III's mental illness, although it is worth pointing out that the notion he suffered from Porphyria, a genetic blood disorder, is probably untrue. That belief gained traction in the 1960s, and certainly, there is evidence of the condition running through the royal bloodline. But its original proponents were arch monarchists, keen to find an alternative to the notion of a madness infecting Royal lines, and their diagnosis was misplaced. In fact, the most likely answer is that he suffered from extreme bipolar disorder. His symptoms – being a King, they are well recorded – seem archetypical. He probably experienced his first bout of that condition when he suffered unexplained illness, around the age of fifteen. Then the triggers of the twin deaths of his two young sons so close together send him spiralling into the depression and mania which haunts the remainder of his life.

Undoubtedly, the deep divisions which grew between himself and Parliament added to his distress. These are so bad that in 1783 Parliament condemned his influence as a 'high crime'. Yet despite all the problems, the Industrial Revolution is turning Britain into the most powerful and richest nation on earth. A new middle class is emerging, a group whose wealth can rival that of the traditional elite, the landowners and aristocracy.

The old ways still hold sway; these powerful middle classes ape the actions of people who consider themselves their social superiors. But, and that is a word essential in any examination of the Regency, these middle-class upstarts are also bringing about change. They will not be downtrodden.

Meanwhile, Britain's empire is expanding fast. By the time of the Regency, Britain's representatives in Asia, the East India Company, were out of control. Its practices are dire, cruel and exploitative. It needs taming. Both Parliament and George agree on that. However, the shackles Parliament wishes to employ are of a kind that are politically the opposite of the ones George wants to see. More tension. More unrest.

This backdrop is important because it plays a significant part in the emergence of those traits we associate with the Regency period. And up there with the most important of these, to the Regent at least, is Napoleon.

Maybe the Prince genuinely wants to engage him in honourable conflict. Maybe such a claim is just a pretence to bolster his terrible reputation within the country. Which, thanks to the Regency Act, has suddenly taken on extra importance. Since he chooses not to go to war himself, the Prince must choose his own battlefield. He has already engaged in, and is winning, the war of the arts. He launches an attack in another arena, aiming to defeat his foe in the sartorial stakes as well. The West End tailor, Meyer (and later, his partner Mortimer), provided the extravagant ceremonial uniforms he favoured. And altered them to fit his growing stomach. Waistcoats were lengthened to hide his double chins; jackets expanded to allow them to do up.

We see more of his extravagance and his irresponsibility in the company's ledgers of the time. Copious amounts of golden thread, ribbons and buttons are ordered. Rarely, though, are they paid for. One page totals a debt of more than £490[2], a considerable sum for the time. Equivalent to £30000 today; a significant part of a company's turnover.

Civilian garb was also important. The trendsetter of the time was, unsurprisingly, a man. Beau Brummell. The Regent became obsessed with Brummell's look. If the Regent led, his courtiers would necessarily follow. Men could spend up to three hours a day attempting to replicate the style that had enthralled their leader. Thus the 'dandy' was born. An almost effeminate look which, at the time, was an attempt to accentuate manhood. The point is that fashion – sartorial and artistic – was of huge importance in the Regency era. Maybe it became so because men, and the Prince of Wales, in particular, had been emasculated by Napoleon's soirees in Europe.

Another factor which leads to this period of rapid change is the growth of the press. Not only do newspapers and journals help to inform the people of the lives of the rich and influential, but they also hold them to account. Most notably, of course, Parliament and the monarchy.

But the time is not just about political matters. The growth of both the London and provincial theatres has made these cultural centres significant players in the lives of many people. The theatre is a source of entertainment, offering a window into the lives of the rich and landed. The Romantic period of poetry, to many the most important of any literary cycle, is taking hold. New writers are emerging in the world of the novel, and improved printing processes are making books accessible to far more people.

For the elite of society, staying ahead of one's neighbours is vital. One's balconied, balustraded home must have the finest striped wallpaper and the best pastel shades. The largest and most glittering ornaments, crockery and trinkets. Subtlety is not a strong point, and if a neighbour orders a new silver tea service, then your own addition to the family heirlooms will be made of gold. With the insertion of diamonds, sapphires and rubies, too, if finances allow.

The aristocracy sought to protect itself from the growing influence of the middle classes. The Season is the period of the year when the elite gather to show off their finery and enjoy dances, balls and dinners. It is a closed shop, with entry closely guarded and the events used as an opportunity for the aristocracy to strengthen itself. New partnerships between families are formed as young men and women are married off.

The most notable feature of the Regency elite is their dress. Alongside the splendid, almost effeminate, attire for men, long flowing gowns of classical design are in vogue for women. It is a period for taking the air, for parks and squares surrounded by imposing buildings. It is also the time for decorum, for ladies at least. And that decorum is oppressive and restrictive. Yet alongside these controls on women (and others), libertines among the rich, the educated, and the entitled enjoy freedoms perhaps greater than ever before. Life is for enjoying. Provided a thin veneer of propriety is always on show, the elite can get up to pretty much whatever they like. Which usually means lots of sex. Maybe this libertine lifestyle emerges as a direct contrast to the existential threats facing the aristocracy. Threats from overseas and within their own nation. The people are, literally and otherwise, revolting. Nearly, at least.

It is a time not only for social libertines but religious ones as well. George III makes concessions to Catholics; his son will even marry one. Culturally, too, the literary groups, the Quakers and the

Wesleyans, enjoy a period of influence. Even the slave trade, upon which much of the country's wealth is built, is under threat from abolitionists who understand that the practice is just wrong. The King himself allows his public to petition him directly. Most may still not have the vote, but there is a growing recognition that they should have a voice. Yet behind this time of happiness and enlightenment, a different world also operates.

Poverty among the working classes is extreme, disease is rife, and education limited. Intolerance rears its head – when George III makes his concessions to the Catholics, there are riots in the streets. Moral contradictions are everywhere.

It is not the worst time for minorities, but black society, LGBTQ people and foreigners are widely discriminated against. Justice is improving, but not for the poor, and many are sent overseas to Australia to populate the colonies. Their crimes can be as little as stealing a morsel of bread. Sex clubs, bawdy dens of iniquity, and prostitution are all rife and frequented as much by the rich as the poor. In fact, even more so because the rich have the means to exploit these sordid opportunities. The stench of bodies permeates; bathing is a rarity, and diseases such as syphilis are widespread.

Misogyny exists everywhere. To be a woman in the Regency times is to be expected to follow a strict and unwavering set of conventions, and to break them is to bring down the ire of society. Yet, for all this, it is a time of hope and change. Many women do make a difference and break through the glass ceiling of this man's world. Rights and liberties are greater than before and indeed are wider in some ways than in the Victorian era, which will soon follow.

Certainly, life for a poor person is unimaginably different to that of a rich one. In every way, from the education received to their life chances and expectancy to the food they eat, the clothes they wear and the entertainments they enjoy. Even as specific as the time a person gets up. A labourer is there at the crack of dawn to work a hard day's labour for a pittance. A rich person, on the other hand, may find their day starts late, and for entitled women, in particular, the word 'morning' means 'after noon'. Literally.

This incredible period in British history is littered with contradictions, breakthroughs, traditions and beauty. It is a time of opportunity, advancement, decadence and excess. We will examine it and do so through the eyes of women, especially those who broke past the expectations of the time and made a difference in their own ways.

CHAPTER 1

CRIPPLING CONVENTIONS: THE RULES OF ROMANCE

Imagine the following challenge. Try to pick out one significant change for women which occurred during the Regency period. That is quite a task. There are so many facets to women's lives which moved forwards – and occasionally backwards - during that brief period. Perhaps though, if pushed, there is something which stands out more than any other single change. Something which remains topical for the times we live in today.

Because suddenly, without any noticeable reason why, women were able to say 'No.' No to marriage, no to the advances of a man. No to the wishes of their parents. Imagine that.

In the eighteenth century and before, matters had been very different. Take marriage as a pertinent example. Then there were so many reasons to enter into wedlock. Marriage for money... a wise move; marry for status... why not? Marry for business, or before it is too late. All legitimate reasons for tying the knot. Marry for love? Well, if you have to. It wasn't illegal. Such a situation was not even considered wrong. But romance was merely one of several reasons why a couple may become legally bound. Commonly, the bond was forged by parents as much as by any love which grew over time. Certainly, that was and had been, the case among the middle classes, the gentry and the aristocracy. But by the turn of the nineteenth century, such practices were disappearing fast. They were not completely gone. Change doesn't occur that quickly. Many factors still contribute to a wise marriage. Simply though, love, mutual attraction and romance had made their way to the fore. For a woman, no longer must she accept a proposition because it was the sensible thing to do or because her parents (often the father) wanted it so. More likely, she would marry because she wanted to.

Perhaps a factor which played its part was that those conditions under which love, as opposed to business, might blossom were far more attractive than they had used to be. The Regency period can be characterized by sparkling social events, stunning architecture, unique and immediately notable decoration and fashion. Everything was designed to entertain the young and not-so-young. At least, that was the case for the rich, the titled and the landed. It certainly did not apply to ordinary women.

Not that we should oversimplify. Marriage was still a complex matter governed by unwritten rules and conventions which must be followed. It was still not an equal partnership. Not even close to that. The man took the lead, and the lady followed. Suppose that was what she wanted. The difference was that she could, at last, say no. Say it with the hope, and frequently the prospect, of being heard.

But if conventions were changing, they remained strong throughout the period. By the onset of the Regency, the process of marriage became much more fluid, more natural, and more in tune with human feelings. That is not to say that the stages of the process remained anything but clearly defined. And even if progress towards greater equality was happening, the onus towards romance still lay with the man. It was he who was expected to be proactive, while his subject for adoration allowed matters to develop around her. It all sounds deeply romantic.

Picture the scene. An elegant room decorated in striped wallpaper and chandeliers. There is music and wine. The men are dressed as peacocks, the women stunning in their pure white gowns. The shape of the layers of thin material enhanced the natural contours of their bodies, tightly gripping in places, flowing like the soft branches of a weeping willow elsewhere. Beauty is everywhere. Of course, it was not like this in the slums of the cities or even in the chilly homes dotted through bleak villages. Not even among the new middle classes, some of whom would see their own wealth challenge that of the aristocracy. But among the gentry, it was thus. It is these lives which are celebrated in history, which are still what we visualise when we picture the Regency era. This book will also look at the lives of ordinary women and of the new middle classes rising on the back of industrialisation. But not yet.

It is the role of the woman to be wooed and the man to take the lead. The woman to be the object of desire, and the man to flatter. Archetypically romantic. To some. Others might see it differently. Such a system makes the lady the passive partner in a burgeoning relationship. The man the active one. But it is as it is, and at least both partners now played a significant, primary and decisive role in the fulfilment of their lives.

The first step on the road to matrimony is to be invited to key social events. For a woman, this might not always be as easy as simply belonging to the right family. Although, that definitely helped. A young lady must be regarded as sound. Despite all the progress of the period, gender stereotypes still dominate. The lady must be demure, coy even, and ensure she does not break with convention. For men, there is much more leeway. Drunkenness, lechery, and crudity are all, if not exactly welcomed, accepted as a part of what it means to be a man.

It would be naïve to believe that parents, aunts, grandmothers and uncles never played a part in organising this first meeting. Not only in arranging the dinner, or the dance or ball but also in carefully considering who to invite. A whole spider's web of interactions would occur to ensure that the right people would be present. This was the hostess's job, and the best did it superbly well. To be a successful hostess was to hold supreme influence over future liaisons. Certainly, that is the case among the upper classes, where there remains a strong reason to ensure that young adults marry wisely. And by wisely, we mean with financial and social prudence. Where the upper echelons of society led, the next layer down followed. Hence the middle classes too developed their own conventions towards marriage which mirrored those of their social superiors. The middle class, though, was new and changing. A state of flux existed here. Driven on as the body grew outwards from the professions to include the new, super wealthy factory owners and their managers.

Once the leading actors are present at the important event in the social calendar, the pre-courtship stage will follow. Thus, a family will often steer a son towards a certain lady in the hope that a spark will light. Equally, they will try to ensure their daughter attends events where a particular young beau will be present. No longer, in the main, could they simply introduce a couple having already made arrangements between themselves as to what that outcome will be. Although through complex machinations, they will seek to achieve the same outcomes.

Convention dictates that in this pre-courtship stage, it is the man who makes all the moves. But if we discover anything about the Regency period, it will be the significance of appearing to do the right thing in public while acting as you wish behind the scenes. A time of moral dubiousness because society was led by the most morally dubious character of all, the Prince of Wales. Therefore where a lady felt attraction towards a man, but he remained ignorant of her charms, she would not attempt to manipulate further meetings. On the surface, the woman would be passive, but behind the scenes, she could be working hard to further the chances of any romance developing.

And so, across a table packed tight with food and decanters of wine, or at a ball with dancing and frivolity, or at a brother's wedding, eyes might meet, and hearts flutter. What next? Well, to be honest, convention once more dictates what activity will follow, which is not a lot. Certainly not actual courtship. That remains a way down the line. On rare occasions, perhaps after a second or third meeting, a man might approach the lady in question and profess his passion. Although even to move with that small degree of momentum was a rarity and could be considered a tad uncouth. A more traditional route would be to identify the maiden's father, perhaps offer him entertainment if the gentlemen's means extended to such, and request, firmly and respectfully, that he be allowed to advance to the courtship stage.

Mostly though, a man struck by love will simply rely on chance and the steering of whatever good fortune falls his way to ensure more encounters occur. He will hope that the flame might gain strength and be certain of spreading enough to light that second candle. All very romantic, indeed. And rather sweet. But as for a woman who fell for a man. Society dictated that she could do nothing, and must await the next step, hoping that her feelings are mutually held. She certainly is not expected or even, according to good society's rules, permitted to become the hunter. Although, as we have seen, just because society dictates it does not mean that the woman must follow. At least, not in private.

But what of ordinary people? If love blossomed slowly for the ruling classes and with much adherence to unwritten rules, how did the young of the labouring class proceed? Much less information is available regarding the etiquette of romance for the lower classes. However, we can draw conclusions from the commentators of the day. One of the most significant of these is the painter Joseph Mallard William Turner. What makes Turner such a valuable source is that he paints what he sees. These images are then recorded for posterity.

The unfortunate (for the British) happenings across the English Channel played a huge part in the lives of the Regency rich. No longer could they travel across to mainland Europe to experience the architecture, fashions and culture of their European neighbours. The result was that people looked inwardly for their inspiration. Called the picturesque, a movement grew to celebrate the beauties of the British countryside. Bucolic scenes of ruined abbeys sitting atop sweeping valleys. Babbling brooks with children dancing joyfully across flat stepping stones. That sort of thing. England of the late eighteenth and early nineteenth century featured such scenes in abundance. If the rich and adventurous could not get their cultural fill across the Channel, they sought the next best thing. And that was considered to be the counties of Dorset, Wiltshire, Somerset, Devon and Cornwall. Here the picturesque was everywhere. Thus Turner was commissioned to produce a series of paintings of the South West of England to reflect the beauty of the area.

William Turner had an astonishing eye for detail. One of the most telling works he produced on this tour is 'Plymouth, from Mount Edgcumbe'[3]. Not only does Turner catch the contrast of beauty in the foreground and the threat of war and danger in the distance, with warships anchored in the harbour, but he is also happy to share his interpretation of everyday lives.

So he captures a number of sailors who have presumably enjoyed a day of shore leave. Now they are dancing back to the harbour, arm in arm, with several women dressed in simple white dresses and bonnets. It seems likely that the couples have met either on the day or the night before. Still, the physicality of their engagement is way beyond what would be considered polite or appropriate among the higher classes. There is clearly merry-making taking place. A sailor dances with his violin, his demeanour indicative of men having a very good time. Others are moving under the relaxed influence of post-coitus charm.

We can infer that the expectations of the middle, upper and aristocratic classes were different to those of the working class. These people would not indulge in such open celebrations of their pleasure.

With the pre-courtship stage completed, next came official courtship. There are two significant elements here which demonstrate that the Regency is a time of social advance. Not always, admittedly, advance in the right direction, but movement nevertheless. Firstly, courtship could not begin until the man had proposed to his love. If the lady accepted and became her man's fiancé, then courtship received the green light. Safe in the knowledge that marriage was on the horizon. Not that this means a relationship can get physical. At least, not very. Perhaps a gentle hand on a shoulder or even the careful entwining of fingers. Nothing more. Certainly not the level of interaction Turner's sailors display with their womenfolk.

Naturally enough, theory and practice were often distant cousins. The sensibilities of men and women are far less picturesque than convention demands and perhaps that this expectation of propriety was so severe it accounts for the fact that affairs were commonplace, both in and out of wedlock. We'll come to these in a bit more detail later, but as with so much else, such illicit liaisons reflected the attitudes of the Regency period. Publicly, propriety was all, and such relationships were considered disreputable in the extreme. Privately, as long as they were discrete, nobody cared much — except, perhaps, the women and, occasionally, men, who were being cheated on. Still, since they were probably engaged in their bit of rumpty tumpty, too, things tended to work out equably in the end.

After all, the Prince of Wales was involved in numerous simultaneous liaisons of greater and lesser commitment. One can hardly criticize a prince (although, conversely, many of the time did). And his behaviour set the lead.

Normally, a man will ask his potential bride's father for permission to propose. But he does not have to. He does, however, have to ask his soon-to-be – hopefully – fiancé for her hand. This was the difference the Regency brought to relationships. Prior to the end of the eighteenth century, many marriages were arranged, set in place while sons and daughters were still children, and organised with only a passing reference to the wishes of the participants. That expectation is reflected in the law regarding consent which held legal sway right up to the Marriage Act of 1753. A woman could be married at fourteen. A man – boy more appropriately – at just twelve years of age. The Regent himself was believed to be involved in numerous sexual encounters before he was fifteen. However, following the Act, a condition was added that where the participants were under the age of 21, parental permission must be sought and granted. In theory, this would stop the exploitation of young women and, sometimes, boys. Although, since most exploitation had a financial basis to it, and it was the parents who would often benefit directly or otherwise, such a condition was largely ineffectual. Maybe that was why, by 1823, this notion of consent had been removed, and once more only became required if the participants were under the ages of twelve and fourteen, respectively.

As laws go, the Marriage Act did little to protect the people it claimed to defend. Parents were most often making the decisions about who a son or daughter would marry, and actually increasing the age at which a couple could marry without explicit permission served to take decisions even further away from the participants. It did, however, raise the concept that children and young people have rights, and maybe it was that which, forty years or so on, led to the couple themselves having the ultimate say as to whether they actually married.

Further, during the Regency, a woman could quite legitimately say 'No' to a proposal and do so without fear of damage to her reputation. Well, sort of. Jane Austen herself noted, in a letter of March 1816, that 'Single Women have a dreadful propensity for being poor, which is one very strong argument in favour of matrimony.'[4] So it follows that a woman may certainly reject the proposal of a suitor; whether she would be wise to do so to too many gentlemen is another matter.

However, for our story, let us assume that the question has been popped and an affirmative given. What next for our not-yet-permitted-to-be amorous couple? Again, the answer is a little disappointing. Since the relationship had a proper footing, certain allowances are now made. Gifts can be exchanged; affectionate touching – hand holding, an arm around a shoulder and so forth – are now officially tolerated, provided they are discrete. More time may be spent in each other's company. The couple can get to know each other. Platonically, at least. This might seem a bit late since the two are by now already committed to marriage. Unsurprising, many relationships failed to even survive to this point.

A lady, though, must have a chaperone present during any encounter with her husband-to-be. Undoubtedly, this is a condition held more in expectation than reality. Since time began, couples in love have found ways to be alone. The same must be true of the Regency period. Again, though, discretion is all.

But if some elements of choice and romance are now a part of the marriage process, finance still lays close to its heart. This is not to suggest that prior to the Regency, marriages were no more than a contract meant to provide financial benefit. Of course, many couples were still in love or grew to love one another. But now, such love was a pre-requisite, not a bonus at least until marriage became a necessity to avoid poverty.

Where parental consent is needed, and often even if it is not, lawyers will draw up a settlement contract which, it has to be said, takes away some of the joy of a Regency romance. Or, at least, it puts it into perspective. Parents, and especially fathers, were the drivers of the details of these contracts. Typically, they would cover a number of matters, all of which were directly or otherwise, related to finance.

There is the dowry, which is provided by wealthy families for their daughters. Often this sum is public knowledge. After all, a large dowry means you are doing well as a family. That is not something to keep secret. It also means that your daughter's hand is likely to be more appealing to a wider range of men. Such a system led, of course, to many marriages based on convenience and economics rather than love. So, although conditions are better for women than before – for the richer ones, at least –they are still far from perfect. Next on the list of conditions is a settlement contract for pin money. This is an allowance, usually annual, which is given to the wife while her husband remains alive. As the name suggests, it is meant to cover the basic essentials of life. The wife's wage, we might conclude.

Less common among the conditions of a settlement is any formal allowance intended for future children. This might include the provisions for a daughter's dowry, for example. Finally comes the death settlement. This jointure covers where a wife might live, her allowance, her properties and so forth, which will become hers on the death of her husband, should he pre-decease her.

Meanwhile, alongside the dowry, any possessions of the wife immediately become the property of her husband upon marriage. Given the tendency of the rich to over-indulge in food and wine, participate in endless affairs, and often, go to war, it can be seen how important it is for a woman to secure a good settlement. Otherwise, upon the probably early death of her husband, she could find herself penniless and homeless. Her children too.

The romance of the Regency era is significant. It is certainly a more central part of marriage than in the periods which ran either side of it. But it is not the be-all and end-all of life. And in the background lays the most unromantic element of all. The law. Once committed to marriage, should either side break the 'contract', they may find themselves facing the courts as their partner pursues a suit called a 'breach of promise'. While these did not always follow the breakup of a relationship, they lay like a snake hiding in the grass, ready to strike should the victim become sufficiently enraged... or fancy a nice payout from their partner.

Why, though, were parents so interested in the marriage their children made? Beyond any wish for their happiness? Young women were required to be exposed to potential suitors. Catching a landed gentleman could lift a family from the borders of the aristocracy to its heart or from the middle-class circuit to the heights of upper-class excess. With such a find, a father's business and family outlook would immediately improve. At the same time, demure debutantes must be protected from the lecherous advances of men. How to manage such a series of opposing requirements? As was, and still is, often the case, society took its lead from the top. Or at least what passed for the top in those days. We shall see that the ambitions of families to rise through the uncertain seas of social strata were rarely met. The upper classes were a closed shop and did all they could to remain as such.

For the most aristocratic of young women, the social season in London lasts for around six months of each year, often coinciding with the Autumn and Winter periods when the wealthy abandon their country homes for the financial and social pull of the city. Such a season offers a practical benefit to the upper classes as well. In effect, it ensures that the market for marriage remains closed to all, bar those who meet the standards expected. Aristocracy will marry aristocracy, the gentry to daughters of the gentry. So, the ambitious father of lower social stock will be unlikely to make the social and business advances he seeks, however much he desires them. For these most entitled of young women, only the most eligible of bachelors would attend the dances and balls at which they found themselves. Interlopers were most definitely not wanted. Equally, such gentlemen (which, to be fair, sometimes they were, in the wider sense) wish to find key character traits in their subject. Primarily, the perfect potential spouse must be from an acceptable family and sufficiently wealthy to add to the gentleman's family's own wealth.

But in all but the poorest of environments, another characteristic is required in a potential wife. Maybe not quite as important as wealth or status, but a woman who is not a virgin is unlikely to find a fresh-faced suitor and may have to seek out a rich but older man. This will restrict her ambitions to becoming just his mistress rather than his wife.

With such complex conventions to follow, it is of considerable wonder just how a lady managed to avoid some social gaff and remain an eligible subject for matrimony. Much was learned from mothers, aunts, sisters and cousins. Again, that is society seeking to perpetuate itself. If a person only learns how to be a good wife to a man of standing through the experiences of her own family, then such a route is limited to those whose families are already in the system, so to speak. However, there were more formal means to learn the conventions of the day. It is of no surprise that manuals as to how a proper lady should dress, act and indeed live her life were commonplace. Perhaps the most famous is the 1811 publication, 'The Mirror of Graces', written by a 'Lady of Distinction'. (Presumably, it was regarded as a trifle common to add one's name to a book on etiquette!) We can draw our own conclusions as to why she wished to remain anonymous. To today's eyes, the content is almost humorous in its conceits and arrogance. But in its day, it was a useful guide as to what a man wanted from his lady. At its heart is the concept that the role of a woman is to please her man. Without doing so, she will fail to attract what the author calls, with no sense of irony whatsoever, 'a well-judging man'[5]. Appearance, it seems, is all. Thus a woman must dress to suit her figure and complexion. She must retain excellent posture. A slouch in the body is, it seems, a slouch in character.

To this end, it was not unusual for a lady to wear a backboard beneath her dress, its tight waist – or in a skirt, the narrow, body-hugging band which sat beneath the chest – helping to hold this uncomfortable accoutrement firm. And just in case the plank of wood should slip, leather straps fastened around the midriff added an additional layer of security. What was bodily comfort compared to the consideration of a straight back?

Indeed, this priceless tome suggests a lady goes further. Dressing well is not vanity but rather a sign of good, honourable character. A woman who takes fashion seriously, who carries herself with deportment and grace, is a woman of virtue. The book omits to say that she is also a woman with the time and means to act in such a way, but then to be fair, the book is not intended for the working classes.

There is within its guidance the unspoken implication that to not wear good clothes, to not move in a manner which requires concentration rather than the practicality of just getting from A to B in order to perform whatever duty is required is a sign of a lack of virtue, a lack of honour. Although actually, it is just an indication that a person is poor and must work for their living or look after their home and their children. And what lady will want to appear like that? Again, we see how the upper classes perpetuate themselves as a closed shop. Not only is the behaviour described in 'The Mirror of Graces' something a working class, and even a lower middle class, woman would have no opportunity to replicate even if she had the means, but it is also an unachievable aspiration. Something to admire but never reproduce.

The book does, however, contain some pieces of useful information. The author, a Lady who has apparently attended the highest courts, both English and 'foreign', points out the three principles through which a lady might retain her 'Beauty, Health and Loveliness'. These are temperance, exercise in the open air and cleanliness. That such obvious traits need to be explicitly stated might indicate that they are not always behaviours that a lady of the time will adhere to.

Behaviour, too, is strictly monitored. We might get the impression that a young lady of a certain class is a pampered, protected person, lacking in individuality and character. No doubt some such women did exist, but for most, the rules must be followed and the conventions observed, despite the subjects own attitudes towards them.

Actually, it is a wonder quite how any relationship managed to get off the ground, especially since the role of parents in pushing such engagements was diminishing all the time. Men were expected to appear cold, however much the flames of attraction were burning inside. Aloof, too. The perfect recipe for starting a romance. Or not. But if men were expected to hide their feelings, then that was nothing compared with how the women of the day were required to act.

A woman is never expected to make the first move, even if it is as innocent and restrained as a glance and a smile. She should be polite and prepared to talk on a wide range of subjects but never, under any circumstances, may she offer an opinion. Most forbidden of all is any suggestion of flirtatiousness. Giving off such a signal could, and most probably would, scar a lady's reputation for life and seriously impact her likelihood of marriage. Once a lady soils her copybook, she will find herself excluded from invitation lists.

In fact, a lady who makes any kind of advance toward a young man without being formally introduced to him faces the prospect of becoming the talk of the town. And not in a good way. As we can see, the entire process of gaining 'an introduction' is fraught with dangers on both sides. Even a lady may not be introduced without her agreement, and then there is the matter of finding somebody of sufficient seniority to garner this agreement to interact from both the man and the lady. Social standing is also a factor. Either side might refuse to speak with a person of a lower status. In fact, such a response was largely expected at the time. How else to ensure the higher echelons remain exclusive?

As we have seen, dances were good ways to get the younger generations to meet, with the intended ultimate outcome of a marriage proposal somewhere suitably down the line. But even at a dance, there was no spying on an attractive potential partner and waltzing in. No, still, the whole formal process of securing an introduction is required. It is hard to imagine how the interested party manages to avoid losing the moment. That moment could be short-lived as well, especially for the lady. It was acceptable for a man to ask for a second dance, an indication that he was interested. But should he try for a third, and the lady agree, it is she who will carry the ultimate stigma of being a flirt, or worse. In such circumstances, a lady will find herself off the invite list for future events, which itself equates to social disaster.

Dinner parties, too, carried their own complex sets of rules. Provided the lady waited to be served, did not initiate a conversation, ate little (whilst always giving the impression of enjoying every course – of which there might be up to twenty-five!) and did not get drunk or slurp her soup, she would probably be OK. It seems as though the idea that a dinner party might actually be enjoyable, for a young, unbetrothed lady at least, is a fallacy.

Even once an introduction has been made, the lady must not display any emotions. She may laugh at a joke, but politely and in a restrained way. And certainly not if the language involved is vulgar. (It was fine, naturally enough, for men to jest as inappropriately as they wished, provided they did so out of the way of sensitive ears. Although, such ears did not extend to women of the streets. Those of lower social standing can be as vulgar as they wish.) But with a nice degree of hypocrisy, while a woman is expected to keep her emotions in check, it is acceptable to experience a 'fit of the vapours'. In other words, to faint when in earshot of foul language. There is little medical science to suggest ear sight of an obscenity can bring about unconsciousness, but the sight of a lady fainting was a sign of her sensitivity. And, therefore, purity. More likely, the corsets which promoted their wearers' 'Empire Waists' and the backboards which kept them upright were not only uncomfortable but unhealthy as well. Bouts of light-headedness would be both commonplace and unavoidable. A far more likely reason for the onset of the vapours than overhearing a reference to bodily functions.

Ladies of the day even needed to watch their behaviour when out about town. It was perfectly acceptable, provided an introduction had been made, to walk and converse with an acquaintance or even a stranger but never to stand still when doing so. And a lady must be aware of who she passes. To cut a person to whom she has been introduced is to incur a stain on her character that no amount of careful cleansing will remove.

There was one rule that, when it came to finding romance, was a little easier to follow. A rule which can be expressed in a single word. Don't. Don't find yourself in the presence of another man unless you have a chaperone with you. The exceptions to this rule were extremely restricted; being married or over thirty (and therefore, assumed to be worldly enough to avoid corruption) usually being the only excuses for such behaviour. The chaperone issue was a challenge as well. Another lady is fine, as is a male relative. A husband is fully acceptable, and at a push, even a servant can pass muster. However, walking with a gentleman to which a lady is not attached is seriously dicing with death. So don't. Even if no ulterior motives on either side exist. Just as bad, though, is walking alone. Again. Don't. Certainly, a lady may walk alone to church, or if strolling on her morning exercise (taking the air being a sign of a proper upbringing, as our 'Lady of Distinction' points out), but opportunities for a quick but solitary excursion were extremely limited in Regency times. At least early on in this period because fortunately, 'Don't' was soon to be usurped by 'Perhaps.' A small change, but one in the right direction.

The Regency was a period of rapid change. In itself, a Regency is a highly unusual event, and the one in question here was made even more of a state of flux by the challenges presented by Napoleon's France.

The recent loss of America to independence had been another kick in the teeth for British confidence. Further, the supremacy of Parliament over the monarch was unsettling, even if, on balance, right for the times. When politics are in a state of uncertainty, society changes quickly. Thus, by the end of the Regency, it had become more acceptable for a lady to be seen out alone, and the importance of the chaperone had begun to diminish.

Any lady who did not keep her wits about her could end up committing any number of infringements of etiquette, which made her a social outcast. Being demure, speaking when spoken to, being swept off one's feet by a man and then living a comfortable and petted existence might sound easy enough, provided you were of the social class able to enjoy such privilege. In reality, achieving those goals was more than a challenge.

In fact, we might wonder why a lady put up with such restrictive expectations. The answer is multi-faceted. Even today, we are bred and engineered to follow conventions, to fit in and to know our place. (Which is easier if your place is at the top of the table, so to speak). But there were practical reasons for following the rules in Regency times. The biggest one, for a lady, was to avoid ostracisation from her social class, which would be a fate worse than death. Or, certainly, on a par with it.

A well-heeled young lady would probably never be poor, her family money ensuring her survival. But committing breaches of expectation destroys a reputation, and that is a sanction of the highest order. The breach does not even have to be in public. Even in the privacy of one's own home, standards are expected to be met.

Just, those standards could be, and were often, somewhat contradictory. For all the decorum of the pre-courtship and courtship stages of a relationship, once marriage has taken place and an heir or two provided, it is deemed quite acceptable and even understandable for a lady to find a lover. After all, the chances are her husband is doing the same. The key here is discretion; nobody minded a lady having a lover provided, officially, they knew nothing about it.

Although there was more than a reasonable chance that having had a couple of children, the lady would be in no fit state to indulge in an extramarital dalliance. Because childbirth, or the infections which so often followed, accounted for about one in five female deaths. Unusually, the rich experienced additional risks than those facing the poor when giving birth. (Not that the death rate among the lowest strata of society was anything but considerable. Just, some of the risks were different.) A family with money would more likely employ a midwife and a doctor, while servants would wait on the mother hand and foot. This simply gave more opportunities for contact with people who did not wash their hands. The chances of getting an infection grew in proportion to the number of people around during childbirth and the period immediately after.

Secondly, a woman from a higher-class family would be more likely to be enclosed in a hot, airless room and be required to lay still. This lack of exercise and movement also presented a threat to the expectant mother, as well as her child.

The poor, though, were not without their own challenges when it came to giving birth. Alongside the factors which made them poor in the first place – lack of access to good, nutritional food, lack of adequate housing and so forth, the dirt and squalor in which they lived exposed them to risks of infection as well.

To return to the question as to why women of the era adhered to the suffocating conventions with which they were faced, we only have to read Jane Austen to realise that, in fact, not all women did stick to the rules. Throughout history, people have stood up for their rights and challenged the conventions of the day. The Regency era was no different, and we shall come across many such women in due course.

A second section of the population who eschewed the conventions of the day also existed. For some women, marriage might be an unwelcome prospect, even if a necessary one. These were the members of the lesbian community. Maybe unsurprisingly, given the mores of the time, not much information exists about the gay community of the day, although it seems as though lesbians were treated more leniently than male homosexuals. Still, the same rules applied. Without a husband, a women's options were limited. There was, therefore, almost certainly a stronger gay community than records suggest. Many gay women, we believe, took a husband out of convenience and necessity.

Not though, that one might tell this from the fashion of the day. And fashion was, during Regency times, of the utmost importance.

CHAPTER 2

AN EYE FOR STYLE AND ELEGANCE: REGENCY FASHION

Women's fashion at this time could be as uncertain as the political climate. It underwent great change during the era. For women, dress must not only display elegance, but it also needed practical qualities. To hide corsets and backboards, to disguise the tools of a lady's trade.

In order to understand how fashion developed for women during this period, we must once more cross the Channel and look at what was happening in Napoleon's France. The Emperor was driven by a need for his nation to lead the world. Not only militarily but in terms of culture and fashion as well. But he had a problem. The French textiles industry lay a long way behind its loathed British counterpart. While the onset of the Industrial Revolution led to the development of machinery which could produce fine clothes quickly and, relatively speaking, cheaply, France's own political revolution had hit their textile industry hard. But Bonaparte had some novel ways to try to get it back on its feet. He ensured that the Valenciennes lace industry received significant investment, allowing the manufacture of top-grade textiles such as tulle and batiste. He then ensured that a strong market existed for these goods. Firstly, he banned the import of cheaper (but equally fine) materials from Britain. Then, to ensure that the French industry found customers prepared to spend generously, he imposed the rule that a lady could not wear the same clothing at court more than once. He even went as far as to order the blocking of fireplaces. Thus, ladies would need to wear more layers of clothing to fight the cold.

He also had in his wife, Josephine, the perfect model for the fashions he enjoyed. The slender Empress looked wonderful in the flowing dresses her husband – and therefore designers – favoured. Meanwhile, in Britain, fashion was following a similar line. If we accept that the Regency period, in terms of fashion at least, ran from 1790, then it marked the introduction of the Empire line. This had at its origins the classical chemise style shift, which gathered at the neck and under the breasts, often with a colourful sash tied to emphasise the narrowness of ladies' torsos. Below, the dress was full and flowing. By 1800 a touch of the risqué had entered the equation. No doubt in an attempt to titillate the fires inside men, a low cut and squared-off neckline was added. It is this décolleté that we associate strongly with the era. Indeed, it was not uncommon – and became increasingly popular – for a dress to fall off the shoulder. During a time when outward displays of passion and excitement were frowned upon, such a revelation must have been almost unbearable to hide for both the lady concerned and the man whose attention she had caught.

Again, there was a practical use to this design. A lady was meant to be demure, and that forbade extravagant movement. With their dresses held none too securely around the arms, movement must be dainty and charming. By necessity, if one did not wish to risk losing one's modesty! And one did not.

It was usually the case that the exposed, low-cut neckline was spared by day and saved until a lady might find herself on show at a special event during an evening, such as a dance or ball or dinner party. While the style of flowing Grecian robes dominated during the daytime hours as well as for the evening, in these earlier hours, modesty could be preserved with the addition of a chemisette (a small blouse) to cover the upper chest area. Or perhaps a small piece of lace. That industry was not just limited to Paris. It thrived in the central and eastern counties of England too. Buckinghamshire, Northamptonshire and Bedfordshire were famed for their lace production.

We can get a small insight here into the lives of ordinary people. Somebody like Eliza Payne, who was born in Oakley, Bedfordshire, in around 1816. She spent her life working in the industry. The work is perfect for those unfit for a life in the fields. It is dominated by women, children and men who cannot find employment on the farms. We can tell from this that pay was low, and therefore hours were long.

Eliza would be trained in the skills from as soon as she could hold a needle. Her family had worked with lace for generations. She attends a lace school, where the costs of her tuition are met by the proceeds of what she makes. Any surplus goes into the family coffers. The day is long for a small child – three or four hours in the morning, her small lace-making cushion before her as she sits with a dozen others working on their day's task. The same in the afternoon. Five days a week.

Saturday is a free day. After all, she is still a small child. And Sunday is for church and worship.

Eliza's parents had faced a tough choice. They could pay for her to attend the local school, but for a poor girl from a rural neighbourhood, education served little point. The penny-a-week education cost was a poor substitute for their daughter learning a trade – a family trade at that. And if she could earn a little at the same time…

Lace-making is highly skilled and extremely intense. It requires small, dexterous hands and careful eyes. Later, the product of hours of work will be draped casually around the neck of a wealthy lady, its softness rendering it barely noticeable.

Eliza is a real person. She married William Warwick in 1840. Together they have at least four children. Others may have died and missed the census which would record their brief lives. At least one of those children continues in the lace trade. Another, a son, finds a wife who is also a lacemaker. Eliza died in 1883, aged sixty-three. A good age for a woman of her time and class. She is a tiny footnote in history, and although she does not make a difference to people's lives like other women recorded in this book, it is good that we have the chance to remember and celebrate her.

The favoured material of the day was, for the wealthy, muslin. This light cloth flowed naturally around the body and clung in places, highlighting a lady's gentle curves and the attractive figure of the wearer. Early in the period, there was not a huge difference between evening wear and nightwear, so to speak. Underwear was regarded as an optional extra by some (provided they keep it quiet), but for practical purposes, during a cold winter's night or even a chilly summer evening, some extra layers were required. Up top, this would usually be a corset – not designed for comfort or even modesty, but to keep any stray areas of flesh under control and ensure that movement was stylish and ordered. Tied tightly at the back, these accoutrements required the help of a maid to act as a dresser. Therefore we can see that we are describing the clothing of the rich; those from the higher social strata would have a household of maids and servants, and those from the lower echelons certainly did not.

But if the top part of a lady's modesty was so protected, lower down presented more of a problem. The answer was found in the same underwear that men favoured. The pantaloon. These hefty items served more duties than negating the see-through nature of muslin. They were warm too. Often stretching down to below the knee, or even for a particularly cold evening, the ankle, they were the perfect answer to a breezy British night. Flesh coloured for discretion and body-hugging, they were responsible for the impression that Regency ladies were often naked underneath their robes. Although, sometimes, they were.

While muslin was the favoured material of Empire line dresses, other fabrics were used as well. Silks offered a more expensive alternative, but if a muslin was not to be worn, then most often, similar cotton such as an embroidered lawn or batiste was employed. What these fabrics have in common is their lightness of weight and tendency to flow. Daytime dresses would normally be a gentle pastel shade, but it was de rigueur to wear white at night. Which, of course, presented a challenge. Keeping a sheer, light fabric brilliant white required much care and attention. (Although, the job of cleaning would fall to the servants rather than the wearer). Thus, a white dress also became a symbol of the cleanliness and attention to detail of the lady who wore it. Still, though, the British climate played its part in the choice of fabric. During the coldest times, wearing fine wools, linen or even velvet was considered acceptable. A lady may also wear a petticoat made of flannel or a slip to stop her shivering. After all, the sight of a lady shaking uncontrollably could well be misinterpreted, and that would never do. Yet nothing is ever straightforward in the Regency period. Whilst these pure dresses were beautiful and flattering to wear (not least thanks to the suffocating corsets underneath), they were also nearly transparent. For most, this unintended side effect was neutralised with the use of the undergarments explained above. For others, it was exploited. The more Avant Garde ladies of the day would pick out the most transparent of materials, ending up with a dress which gave a tantalising glimpse of what lay, unprotected, underneath. Society was scandalised, and shocked commentators referred to the trend as the 'age of undress'.

As unadulterated and beautiful as it can be, there is a problem with a pure white dress. It's a bit, how to put it, plain. And not very original. Once more, Britain sought change and looked across the Channel to take its lead. Napoleon's forces were spreading to the far East and Africa. Cultural appropriation followed, with the addition of embroidered borders lending colour and variation to the classic white. What started in France (or, perhaps, not) soon spread to England. Costume became more elaborate, with shawls adorning the classic gown look and even the extravagance of tassels adding mystery and flavour. As is so often the case, initially, such adornments were beautifully embroidered, adding to the beauty and the cost of the item. Soon, though, as demand and popularity grew, the quality of such embroidery dropped. Fashion of the time spread out from the landed classes, and as it reached the new middle class, quantity outstripped quality.

Winter continues to raise its head. Central heating was a notable omission from the horse-drawn cab of the Regency period, and a coat would be required to keep a person warm. The Pelisse became the garment of choice during the era. Trimmed with fur, cut straight and made of a warm material, this coat evolved between 1800 and 1850. For a time, just below knee length was the fashion, later, the coat extended to full length. But as with dresses of the age, the Pelisse was a flowing garment which hugged the chest and often the hips, accentuating the wearer's shape. At other times, it was fuller. Accompanied by some form of hat or bonnet, it became the emblem of wealth, class and style.

And practicality. Prior to the emergence of the Pelisse, the best a lady could do to keep even moderately warm was to don a short Spencer jacket. These cut-off toppings were actually bastardised forms of the Spencer coat men had begun to adopt. Apparently (but not definitely), Earl Spencer had stood with his back too close to his fire. As a result, the long angular tips of his jacket ignited, somewhat burning his dignity. Ever the practical man, the Earl decided against the simple solution of standing a little away from the fire and instead had his coattails removed. The result was a kind of semi-jacket which ended at the middle of the back. Ladies began to adopt the style as a sort of inefficient cardigan, which provided little protection from the cold. The arrival of the Pelisse must have been most welcome.

The Spencer did not go completely out of style, at least not until about 1820. Instead, it evolved into a light coat made of wool or silk and known as a kerseymere. Lighter, silk versions became evening wear accoutrements, and here went by the name of the Canezou.

Maybe as a reflection of the time, or perhaps as a nod towards the Prince of Wales's delight in dressing up in military garb, these jackets were often finished off with braid or tassels, giving them a slightly military look. In fact, this eventually evolved into the Hussar jacket, which was a kind of ladies' military-style evening wear.

By the time Parliament passed the Regency Act in 1811, the move towards female liberation – of the most tenuous, minimal order, of course – was underway. If it were not enough that a lady may now turn down the attentions of an unwanted gentleman (or other...) and decide for herself who she would marry, the importance of comfort became a growing issue. Growing, but still very small. Whatever, short steps lead to bigger strides.

The body-hugging corsets of the earliest part of the nineteenth century really were uncomfortable and extremely unhealthy. Changes in attitudes did not go as far as to permit a lady to wear clothes in which she could feel truly at ease. Still, this item of underwear did at least become better shaped, with panels to accommodate the fact that not every lady was shaped like an elongated hourglass. In turn, this softer bodice also allowed for a broader line across the shoulder. The fashion began to change, and it was no longer necessary to be pinned in what was effectively a very stylish, very flattering and phenomenally uncomfortable straitjacket.

Over the next twenty years or so, the classical lines of the early Regency began to become outmoded. Nods to Gothic, Tudor and Elizabethan times became the fashion, with copious trimmings and pleats, rolls and sharply pointed geometric decorations breaking away from the flowing, Greek-style look of the turn of the century.

In the lead-up to the peace treaty with France of 1814, relations between the two powers reached their lowest ebb. This had an impact on English fashion. Simply, designers lost touch with what was happening over the seas. But following the signing of the treaty, travel abroad began to take place once more. What both sides saw was a shock. Most notable, the British waistline had dropped while the French one had risen until it lay almost at breast height.

Consider the sight which met the wealthy of Paris. To French eyes, the British look is ludicrous. The Napoleonic wars might be over, but bad feelings linger, and in this age of satire, French cartoonists take great delight in lampooning the more curvaceous appearance of British ladies of the establishment. British women have to agree, and soon the waistline on their dresses begins to rise, but like a geyser about to blow, this fashion is short-lived. By 1817 the waistline had risen to a level with the breasts – but the following year, it began to drop again until towards the end of this extended Regency period, it lays more or less where it does today.

The short-lived period of comfortable corsets also reached its dying days. As the waistline fell, the need for a tightly packed midriff was felt to be essential once more. Corsets tightened, and women were again put in a position where comfort takes a distinctly second place to looks. The effect is pleasing to the eyes of the time, no doubt. Now, instead of British ladies following France's trends, it became the other way round, and British-style designs became the fashion on the continent too. These lower waist lines did not result in returning to the flowing, classical looks of a decade or two before. Additions such as horsehair are instead used to give a frock substance and allow it to flare out, staying away from the lower legs. At the same time, decorative elements remain. Even frills begin to make a comeback.

It was around 1818 that women decided they needed another style of outer wear to compliment the Pelisse. What followed was the Redingote, a heavier woollen full length almost cape or cloak style coat. This could be worn open indoors to reveal a stylish dress beneath or buttoned when outside to offer fuller protection against the cold.

After all, social events were social events. It was hard enough to break into the privileged circle who attended these extravaganzas, from large-scale balls to elaborate dinner parties. If entry to such events was essential for a young lady seeking a husband, it was equally important for older women to be seen in the right places and to mix with the right people. Their husbands' careers might depend on it. In turn, so would their own spending power.

To receive an invitation to an important gathering is, therefore, of crucial importance to the leading families of the Regency, as well as to those who wish to be considered as such. Certainly, during these times, all events run by the ladies of the gentry, the aristocracy and the upper classes were equal, but some were substantially more equal than others.

CHAPTER 3

BEHIND THE SCENES:
THE WORK OF POLITICAL HOSTESSES

There is a splendid article which appeared firstly in a French publication but somehow made its way into the October 1800 edition of The Lady's Monthly Museum.[6] It is appropriately satirical in style, as was the way of the times on both sides of the Channel. However, whether the targets of its irony are the French, men or, as it purports, female politicians is harder to ascertain with any certainty.

But whatever, taken at face value, it is a remarkable set of observations regarding those women who might claim to hold some political insight towards the times. Contrary to popular belief, some women could, and very occasionally did, vote in Britain right up to the 1832 Reform Act (an act of Parliament that reformed little except to ensure misogyny was firmly established in the statutes). However, the article provides insight into male attitudes of the time. The article was translated (it seems) and published in an English magazine, albeit one aimed squarely at women. This shows that the views within were certainly held by large parts of allegedly educated and entitled male society, even if female readers were being encouraged to lampoon the sexist views.

Women are, variously, and according to the article: likely to bring about 'shameful abuses', somewhat stupid, in the habit of acting above their station (thus being in need of a change in their attitudes), full of injustice, likely to use seduction to get their way, incapable of 'discerning true merit' and 'highly captivated by every thing that tends to dazzle...them.'

They are easy to take advantage of since all they wish to do is please, and they are incapable of prudence. They are cutthroat and prone to greed. In conclusion, the article states, 'It is almost always by them that venality and injustice begin in a state.'[7]

Nice.

What the brief biographies outlined in this chapter will show is that, far from being agents of the devil, women could be great politicians, capable of bringing about change and doing much good for both their families and the nation.

We could be selective here and just show Regency women at their political best. But to ensure balance, we will start with a review of a lady who could easily be a target for ridicule and satire. And indeed she was. But also a woman whose determination to do all for her family and husband saw her have an influence on maybe the greatest military engagement in British history, certainly up to the D-Day landings more than 130 years later. Albeit not the influence for which she might have wished.

A caricature of Charlotte Lennox (1730, or thereabouts, to 1804), the larger-of-life Duchess of Richmond, appears in the National Portrait gallery. 'Are we not ganging to lead ye to Graze on the banks o' the Tweed?' asks the brightly attired, red-faced Duchess of a Bedfordshire bull, small by comparison to the great lady and making its way post haste towards the distance. The Duchess is carrying a large blue ribbon with the word 'Matrimony' emblazoned upon it.[8]

The Gordon Knot, as the picture is known, also has three of the Duchess of Richmond's daughters in the background, one not too tastefully displaying her knickerbockers. A fourth daughter urges her mother to catch the bull. The point of the caricature is that the Duchess had garnered quite a reputation for ensnaring catches for her daughters. Contrary to the usual ways of the day, the young ladies came with little in the way of a dowry.

Clearly, Charlotte Lennox was a lady used to getting her way. Even more notorious than with her endeavours towards her daughters' matchmaking, she even once managed to almost cause a British defeat at perhaps the most famous battle of them all. Waterloo.

Charlotte held aspirations beyond her financial status. The Fourth Duke of Richmond, her husband, was not a wealthy man in terms of the aristocracy of the day. As a result, the Richmonds had followed a well-worn path to Brussels, a sort of cut-price home-from-home for the aristocracy who couldn't quite live up to the social rounds required of such a status. Although to be fair, her husband also carried out some military duties in the European city. Brussels might be seen as a kind of Ascot to the nation's Windsor. Nice enough, close at hand, full of the sort of people you'd like to invite to your party but not, how can we put it, quite the real deal. Like the Berkshire town, Brussels could boast its own horse racing track and, even better, a pleasure park. It was a garrison city so it could offer a ready supply of handsome young officers. All of whom were, naturally enough, out to impress their commanding officer, the Duke himself.

In 1814 Napoleon had finally surrendered, been exiled to Elba, and after twenty years of non-stop war, Europe was at peace. Oh, how these cash-strapped aristocrats lived it up in the Belgian city. Then, in February 1815, Napoleon did the dirty and escaped from Elba. Brussels partied on, with even more military gentlemen now landing, ready to smile on the Mannequin Pis. The rich and regal are about to benefit from having even more eligible bachelors to invite to their balls and dances. Meanwhile, the Duke of Wellington arrives to take control of the combined Anglo-Dutch armies, ready to hold fast against any threat the reinstated French emperor might pose.

A dichotomy of almost classical Regency proportions ensues. During the day, the garrison prepares for war. By nightfall, the city parties as though there is no threat at all. Wellington, meanwhile, attempts to ensure both contradictory aspects of life where the rich and titled can thrive. Contemporary reports indicate that the Iron Duke gave almost weekly balls and attended any other entertainment taking place. Soon it would be the turn of the Duchess to be the hostess, and even though rumours suggested a build-up of French troops on the Belgian border, the Duke was not to be put off by any prospect of having to do his job. 'Duchess,' he said, 'You may give your ball with the greatest safety without fear of interruption.'[9]

Mind you, the Duchess would not have wanted to hear anything else. And remember, she was pretty used to snagging the odd bull, however hard it tried to get away. This particular bovine, though, had every intention of enjoying the fun. It was highly unlikely he would get saddled with any uncertain beauty now, as great a catch as he might be. Battle could be postponed to another day. After all, Charlotte's husband, The Duke of Richmond, Charles Lennox, was the man charged with the responsibility of protecting Brussels from French invasion. Surely any immediate threats were being overstated if he was happy for his wife to organise a party?

So, two hundred of the leading lights in Brussels at that time gathered. Princes, officers, leaders, all. Ready to feast, party, and drink in the face of the imminent invasion. June 15th spread easily into June 16th as midnight passed, and still, the frivolities continued. Then a party pooper of the highest order entered the frame. A messenger carrying the unwelcome news that Napoleon's troops had entered Belgian territory.

Dressed in bright scarlet uniforms – all the better to hide the blood so many were about to fatally spill - worse for wear from wine and brandy, the party ended, the Duchess apparently standing at the door pleading with her guests to remain. Battle could wait another day; there was a further course to serve. The Iron Duke himself, apparently, stated that it seemed Napoleon had stolen a march on him. It was not good form to invade a country while the protectorate was enjoying a glass of the finest claret. Not how a gentleman behaved. But what could you expect from the French?

Of course, all worked out for the best. If the British and Dutch forces could not hold off the French invasion at Quatre Bras, then shortly afterwards, their own literal Waterloo would follow. Even a determined Duchess with a party to complete could stop that event. Although, thanks to the power of her parties, she did manage to delay it.

In fact, Charlotte Lennox was far from atypical in her endeavours to do the best for her family. Elizabeth Milbanke, later to become Elizabeth Lamb, Viscountess Melbourne, typifies the lengths a mother of the time will go to in order to promote her own family's chances. Not many end up the mother of both a Prime Minister and a Prime Minister's wife. But then, politics was in Elizabeth's blood. Her father was a leading Yorkshire politician, as well as a substantial landowner. (The two tended to go together in those times.)

She married Sir Peniston Lamb aged just 17. That was in 1769. The rapid change the Regency brought was still a distant light on the horizon. Sir Peniston would soon gain the title Viscount Melbourne and eventually become a baron. She had six children, and in line with the mores of the day, the first was with her husband... the remainder were probably not because Elizabeth was a charmer of the highest order. A fine hostess, indeed, the leading Whig hostess of her day – a title she fought hard to retain. When the Duke of Devonshire married Georgiana Spencer in 1774, she saw her place on the podium was threatened. But her political upbringing had served her well. Elizabeth knew when to fight and when to embrace, and this was a time to smother an opponent with friendship rather than spear them with a sharply cut canape. She became the perfect confidante to the new Duchess, whose own relationships were frequently troubled. This, in turn, enhanced her own position in high society.

In fact, being a confidante was possibly Elizabeth's greatest single attribute. She eschewed the trend of being demure and frail with which many Regency women were cast. Elizabeth could be crude with the best of them, and gentlemen visiting Melbourne House were comfortable and secure that they could be themselves.

In fact, nothing would get in the way of her ambition to promote her family. Not even her family itself. When it became apparent that William, her second son and most probably the offspring of the Earl of Egremont, was the most likely of her children to succeed in life, she put all her efforts into ensuring he did. Unfortunately, suggesting that William was the strongest of her children says little for her other offspring. William was selfish, lazy and self-indulgent. An epicurean of the highest order. Perfect character traits for the Prime Minister he would later become, perhaps.

It seems that the Viscountess embarked on several liaisons – but she had given her husband a son (also named Peniston, although he died young), so such life choices were acceptable at the time, provided they were discrete. Perhaps most famously, although certainly not uniquely, the Prince of Wales himself became one of her lovers. She was eleven years his majesty's senior, neatly fitting his penchant for older women. Elizabeth was never slow to seize an opportunity, however, securing for her husband the position of Gentleman of the Bedchamber as a result of her affair. The implication here is that Peniston knew exactly what his wife and master were up to since the role was one that would bring him close to the Regent, acting as a companion as well as a servant.

George and Elizabeth also had a son together, named with unpredictable originality, George, with the Prince of Wales becoming Godfather to his illegitimate progeny. Well, he was the boy's father and, certainly in his own eyes, a bit of a God, so why not?

Perhaps the saddest thing was that Elizabeth did not live to see her ambitions for her family truly realised. She died in 1818, years before either William or daughter Emily (born in 1787, she much later married Lord Palmerston) achieved their greatest moments. A shame because both enjoyed the status of significant figures of their era. Emily was certainly her mother's daughter. From the affected 'Devonshire House Drawl', an excessively posh way of pronunciation separated the entitled Whigs from their social opponents on the Tory party, as well as their social 'inferiors' (who included pretty much everybody else) to her engaging and approachable personality.

So it was that Elizabeth ensured her daughter married early and well. Her husband was rich, a peer, a Whig and a man with a good future ahead of him. He also boasted the impressive name of Peter Leopold Louis Francis Nassau Cowper, which made him the fifth Earl Cowper. Unfortunately for Elizabeth, aspiration sometimes got in the way of achievement. In selecting Cowper as her daughter's husband, she managed to pick a man so devoid of personality, speed of thought and ambition that he quickly sank without trace in the political world as did his relationship with his attractive young wife. Apparently, the two rarely, if ever, spoke. Marriage became no more than a show, with not even a pretence of love emerging. Hence Emily followed once more in her mother's footsteps. She did the honourable thing of providing her husband with an heir and then set about embarking on a series of affairs. As with her own siblings, the fathers of her future children have not been recorded for prosperity. Although it seems more than a fair bet, they were not the progeny of the dullard Earl Cowper.

Emily became one of the leading patronesses of Almack's, the social club where anyone who was, had pretensions to be, or wished to be seen. She was widely viewed at the future George IV's court and, like her mother before her, was a hostess of wide renown among Whig circles. The Canningite Whigs included two future Prime Ministers at least, her own brother William and Lord Palmerstone. Their favoured hostess was the irrepressible Emily. It seems as though friendship turned to love, and the future prime minister became another of her gentlemen of close acquaintance. (The Regency period does love a euphemism!)

For propriety's sake, it was only after Cowper's death in 1837 that illicit love became open. By this time, Emily was well into her fifties but as vivacious as ever. (In fact, she would live on to the impressive age of 82.) A suitable period of mourning – two and a half years – followed the death of her unloved husband, and then the young Queen Victoria was prepared to give her blessing to the, by now, relatively elderly couple to tie the knot. If only Elizabeth Lamb were able to look down, or up, from wherever she was resting, it would perhaps have been her proudest moment.

Another who achieved fame as a leading political hostess of her day is Harriet Arbuthnot (born 1783). Although, this lady from the outer reaches of the aristocracy hosted members of the Tory, rather than the Whig, side of the political spectrum.

A telling fact from her life relates to her dowry, which, it seems, was a much greater attraction to her older husband than Harriet herself. Although, since Charles Arbuthnot was approaching fifty at the time, the prospect of a wife in her early twenties presumably appealed as well. However, neither love nor physical attraction was enough to prevent him from writing to his then fiancé and stating: 'How can you and I live upon £1000 or £1200 and Fane (her mother) finds it so impossible to live upon her £6000 that she can offer you no assistance whatsoever?'[10] It seemed that a woman's place was to finance her husband and stand by him. At least in the eyes of the Tory member of Parliament, the Right Honourable Charles Arbuthnot. He was not alone in adhering to such a viewpoint.

For all that, it seems as though the two were happily married, and if affairs were conducted, they were more discrete than most. Certainly, Harriet was a sociable lady who held an (for the time unfashionable) interest in politics and was a great supporter of the Tory party. For these reasons, she was able to engage in some close relationships with political heavyweights of the day, both through her popular parties and personal acquaintances. Foremost among these was her friendship with the Duke of Wellington. Her husband was as close to the Iron Duke as she, which probably indicates that the relationship was platonic. Although, others argue that it had a more romantic nature. That seems unlikely, nonetheless, on the balance of probabilities. The duke was quite open about the unhappy nature of his own marriage, stating that he only wed because 'they asked me to do it' and confirming that he was 'not the least in love with her.' (His wife, that is.)[11]

But his affairs were rarely secret, including when he was Prime Minister. Even in Regency times, a friendship between a man and a woman could be purely social. It's nice to imagine the entitled titled leaping into bed with each other at every opportunity, and many a costume drama has presented life thus, but the reality was, in all probability, a little more mundane.

Harriet died in August 1834, having contracted cholera. It was a sudden, unexpected onset of illness, but she did leave behind a considerable legacy. She was a prolific diarist and her relationship with the Duke of Wellington, alongside her husband's Governmental posts, gave her an insight into the political machinations of the day. They have offered a substantial source of evidence of the fighting between Whigs and Tories of the time and provided the basis of many a historical argument regarding the politics of the Regency and Georgian periods.

Sarah Sophia Fane (1785-1867) was born into substantial wealth. Her mother was Sarah Anne Child, a woman of considerable family money. However, when her father died the year Sarah Anne married into the Westmorland line, it emerged he had decided that his fortune would not be absorbed into this family. Instead, his will decreed that it would pass over Sarah Anne and onto her own child. At the age of 21, that daughter, Sarah Sophia, inherited not only an annual income of £60000 (the equivalent to almost £7 million per annum today) but the grand Osterley Park estate in Middlesex. In addition, as the new senior partner at Child and Co bank, which her family ran, she received significant additional income.

She was also considered a rare beauty. And a fine hostess. Her parties in both Osterley Park and her Oxfordshire estate became must-attend events, the highlights of the social calendar for many. Inevitably, she fell under the eye of two of the great romantic rogues of the day. The Prince of Wales and the poet and womaniser, Lord Byron. Indeed, the Prince ordered her portrait to be commissioned, and when he decided to reject it, Byron offered a letter of sympathy in response. The two would become great friends.

But Sarah Sophia's biggest influence probably came through her position as one of the Lady Patronesses at the aforementioned Almack's Assembly Rooms. The club, located in St James, London, was the social high spot of the country. It had been one of the first institutions of its kind to allow both men and women beyond its doors, and membership was considered a must for anybody wishing to be regarded as a serious player in London society. As a member of the club's committee, Sarah Sophia held significant power over who was granted favour and who was not.

Like those other ladies mentioned above, Sarah Sophia held strong political views and was not afraid to express them. A point that brings into question the established truth that a lady's only political stance should be to have no political stance. Sarah was a committed Whig and openly supported Queen Caroline as George IV divorced her.

Later, she switched allegiance and became an equally staunch Tory. She was a vociferous opponent when the 1832 Reform Act attempted to liberate the voting system in Britain while simultaneously formally disenfranchising women. (Prior to the Reform Act, it was an extremely rare occasion that they were permitted, or chose, to participate in an election, but until that point, nothing was enshrined on vellum to define voting as a male pastime. Perhaps it was because women like Sarah were beginning to express views that led the men of Parliament to be explicit in disenfranchising them.)

In 1804, the strong-willed Sarah Sophia married Viscount Villiers, who would become the 5th Earl of Jersey. George Villiers even took a royal license to add his wife's family name, Child, to his own. But Sarah Sophia appeared to hold a social conscience as well as social status. As she became older, especially after her husband's death, she withdrew from society, although she still regularly received visitors. She also set up schools for those who lived on her Oxfordshire estates and took a considerable interest in improving the conditions in which her workers and tenants lived.

After her death, the diarist and aristocrat Henry Greville wrote: 'Few women have played a more brilliant part in society, or have commanded more homage, than Lady Jersey.'[12]

She was buried next to her husband in Middleton Stoney, Oxfordshire. There to share eternity as, unlike many of their peers, the couple had shared their life on earth. With love and loyalty.

For all that, we might sometimes question the moral decisions of some of the political hostesses who dominated the social sets of the Regency. But we should not forget that a woman's life could be hard. Men held all the cards, and a woman must use every trick at her disposal to become a significant player.

These ladies also add a shade of colour to our understanding of the period. Quite rightly, in an earlier chapter, we outlined the expectations and conventions of the day, especially when it came to women of social standing. The picture we created then was accurate. It describes the position of ladies who were still subject to the conditions in which their own mothers grew up, but who were beginning to find a voice. A quiet voice, rarely more than a whisper maybe… but a say in their futures, nevertheless.

What the lives of the ladies we have outlined in this chapter show is that women could be strong. They could become influential, powerful figures in their own right. They could challenge men and, if they were wily and determined enough, become influencers of their own day.

Women remained in the shadows, dressed in their flowing gowns with tight waistlines and do-not-speak-unless-spoken-to conventions. But not completely. Some, we have seen, were able to cast shadows of their own. Significant ones at that.

And it was not only in the arts that women could make their mark. The same applied to the arts, and it is here that we will turn next.

CHAPTER 4

FROM AUSTEN TO SHELLEY: THE REGENCY'S FEMALE AUTHORS

To be a successful female writer in Regency times. It is hard to think of a more contradictory career. Firstly, of course, a writer must be able to read and write, which limited the field to the middle and upper classes. It was unusual indeed for a working-class woman to have received even the most basic of educations.

But even for the higher classes, convention and expectation weighed down creativity. It was fine to write and even publish a journal, provided it did not say anything controversial. It was acceptable to produce a book which reinforced the rules of the day, literally through a handbook or creatively through a work of fiction. But say something new? Or challenging? Or, horror of horrors, un-lady like? Not a chance.

This meant, in effect, it was just about OK to write something totally uninteresting and unoriginal, which nobody would want to read, but not to produce a work that challenges its audience...and therefore interests them. Which is, subtly, another way to ensure women remain in their place. There are few options for women who have something to say and the skills to say it creatively, in written form. One is to pretend to be someone else, another to just go ahead and bear the ire of right-thinking, male society.

'She was known to the public,' wrote the obituary writer of the London edition of The News, 'as the authoress of a small volume of poems...' All fine so far, although posterity would not remember Charlotte Dacre for her poetry as much as the other writing she published. But then this brief account of her death, published on November 14th, 1825, takes a strange turn. 'And also,' it continues, 'as the writer of certain namby-pamby productions.'[13] We might gather an important conclusion from that dismissive account of the life of one of the leading writers of her day. Being taken seriously is tough for a woman.

Largely, this is because the prevailing view is that it is not a women's place to write. And certainly not to publish[14]. To do so is to bring down the disapproval of society.

Charlotte was born in 1772 (some sources say 1771), the daughter of John and Sara King. Hers was a strict Jewish household, and indeed, John, who was both a writer and a moneylender, was referred to as the 'King of Jews' in his daughter's obituary.[15] In fact, the name Dacre is a pseudonym under which the poet and author composed her works. Something not unusual for a time during which a woman in the public eye might wish to hide her true name.

Charlotte lived during a time when women were expected to be demure and genteel. She was anything but. She tackled big themes in her writing: love, sex and lust. Hardly appropriate material for a lady! Indeed, a topical review of the day said she must have 'maggots in the brain'[16] to come up with such inappropriate (for a woman) ideas.

Dacre began her writing career by publishing a volume of verse called 'Trifles of Helcion' in 1798. However, it was her first novel, 'The Confessions of the Nun of St Omer', which drew her to public attention. The story concerns the repression faced by women during her time, particularly sexual repression. Her edgy subject matter continues. In 'Zofloya' (also known as 'The Moor'), she creates a Gothic tale of murder and horror, as a woman violently kills her rival. However, despite the untimely content she creates, a moral theme runs through her works. Sort of. Her stories focus on the dangers a woman might face. If, that is, she is consumed by lust. But as critically as she was regarded by those in authority at the time, it seems as though Charlotte found favour among the great poets of the day. Both Shelley and Byron were fans, and the close-to-the-knuckle subject matter she produced was an inspiration to them.

1806 was a big year for Charlotte, as not only did she publish her best-known work, but she also married. Her husband was Nicholas Byrne, the editor of The Morning Post newspaper. The paper published some of her earliest poems, which she wrote under the name of Rosa Matilda. Her marriage, though, had been a long time coming. She and her husband already had three children from an ongoing affair when they finally tied the knot, having waited with due propriety until the death of his previous wife.

Like some before her, Charlotte Dacre demonstrated that women did not have to follow the expectations of the day. She sold well during her life, although admittedly has become increasingly obscure over the intervening decades. She proved that a woman could tackle aggressive, sexual, and often violent subject matters and that a female writer's heroine did not have to adhere to the conventions of the times.

It is ironic that her obituary should make reference to 'namby-pamby' works because her stories, despite their underlying morality, were anything but.

Another whose literary talents brought her into contact with Lord Byron is Marguerite Gardiner, who became the Countess of Blessington. Marguerite was born in Ireland in 1789. Early life was typically unpleasant for her, and her father sold her into an abusive marriage when she was just fifteen. She managed to abscond from this suffocating relationship only three months later, sick of the sadistic beatings her husband, Captain Maurice St Leger Farmer, gave out. But it was only after he died violently in an inebriated fight, that she was able to marry her true love. This was in 1817, meaning that the abusive military officer had continued to hold back her life for nearly thirteen years. Such violence was a circumstance under which women of the day were required to live. They could be completely innocent victims in a relationship but were expected to endure that and maintain their public front. The man she married then was Charles Gardiner, who enjoyed the titles of both Viscount Mountjoy and Earl of Blessington.

Despite, or maybe even because of, her childhood experiences, Marguerite matured into a woman of both beauty and wit, one who was generous both financially and with her time and support. She created a salon in London and, from there, became known for her essays about life in London.

If Charlotte Dacre shocked society with her own literary portrayals, Marguerite was regarded more benevolently by those who led Regency society. The Pictorial Times describes her propriety in florid terms: 'To have written and appeared in print was the best proof of a polite and careful education.' The publication goes on to say that the good Lady has 'distinguished herself in the world of letters by prose sketches and miscellaneous poems...'

The presentation might not, though, be strictly true. The earl and his wife had travelled abroad just after the end of the official Regency period and were accompanied by their son-in-law, Count d'Orsa. The young Count, it seemed, was somewhat besotted by Marguerite as was Byron himself. Not that for the not-so-good lord to find himself entranced by a woman is particularly noteworthy. Nevertheless, it seems as though he regarded the 'dewy-eyed' lady as an inspiration during the two months she and her entourage lived with him in Genoa.

But Marguerite's generosity proved to be a problem; before long, her husband's fortune was gone. This became apparent when he died in May 1829. D'Orsay's attraction to his mother-in-law was not just platonic either. As his own marriage broke up, the two remained close

– extremely close – despite the nature of their relationship causing scandal even by the dual standards of the time.

Meanwhile, Lady Blessington (as she was by then) had become a successful writer. She has published the successful 'Memoirs of a Femme De Chambre', recollections of her 'Conversations of Lord Byron with the Countess of Blessingham' and the successful 'The Idler in Italy' and its counterpart based in France. Others, too, including the intriguingly entitled 'Confessions of an Elderly Lady', which emerged early during Victoria's reign. Marguerite may have been a prolific author, but she was also an impoverished one. Whatever income she earned (which, as we shall see when we come to Jane Austen, was never going to be a lot), she spent. To avoid the consequences of her spendthrift nature, she and her younger lover moved to Paris, where they remained for the rest of their lives.

Marguerite is a leading author of her day, accepted and welcomed into good society. Yet even then, she cannot make enough money to survive, despite her husband's relatively substantial fortune. On the one hand, this problem may be a consequence of the challenges women faced even successful ones, during the Regency. Or it may be because she simply could not control her spending. It is hard to determine. In all likelihood, it is a combination of the two that saw her unable to maintain the lifestyle she was familiar with.

This leads us neatly to Frances (Fanny) Burney. If Marguerite's writings were smiled upon by the powers that be, Fanny's certainly did not evoke the same response. Shakespeare talks of the 'balloon reputation', an inflated ego which is wafer thin and so easy to pop. He could have been talking about many of the upper classes of the day. Their protective coating was made up of convention, and that provided merely the thinnest of veneers. Fanny made these narcissistic aristocrats the target of her writing. She pierced them with unforgiving savagery. Her weapon? Satire. And my did she fire her burning arrows with accuracy and force.

Fanny was born in 1752. Her father was a noted musician. Her mother died when Fanny was just ten. It seems that her mother's death was the trigger for her to turn to the page. From the age of twelve, she began to keep a diary, which she entitled, enigmatically, 'Addressed to a Certain Nobody'.

Fanny was a moderately prolific writer and very determined with it. She must have been because out of her eight plays, only one was performed during her lifetime, and that closed after a single performance. Poking fun at our masters and their mistresses was just not cricket, even the primitive form of the game played in those days. However, she also produced no less than twenty-five volumes of journals, a biography and four well-received novels.

Fanny was not afraid to be provocative. Or to take her pen down avenues along which others would not venture. In a way, she was like Charlotte Dacre in this. If Dacre focused on those passions and emotions which women held, then Fanny looked more at the social controls which prevented women from expressing their true selves. She adored firing shots into the pretensions of the aristocracy and equally enjoyed using them to expose women's degraded place in society.

Fanny was, in many ways, the forerunner of more famous writers such as Jane Austen, opening the door to audiences who were becoming familiar with the fact that those with the most inflated opinions of themselves are also those more ripe for puncture. Yet if her writing could be subtly explosive, it seems as though her character was different. Brought up in London – where her father moved after his wife's death – she mixed with the city's cultural elite. Which, in those days, implied the social elite as well. Although apparently very funny when in company with which she was familiar, she was the archetypal demure lady in society gatherings. When her first novel, 'Evelina', was published, her peers may have begun to realise that a truly silent assassin sat quietly within their midst. Silent and secret: reportedly, Fanny wrote in a disguised hand for fear that she could be identified as the author of these devastating works.

Remember, to be a female writer was frowned upon in Regency and pre-Regency times. That her novels were, in fact, well received and popular is a sign of their quality and her well-liked nature. Although that her first book was initially published under the name of her brother James might also help to explain the lack of outrage which initially greeted it. But then, the literary climate was crying out for a breath of fresh air. 'Evelina' provided it.

But even Fanny's father was unaware that his daughter was that novel's author. She was afraid that he would disapprove of his daughter, still a young woman, entering the sordid world of publishing. But Dr Burney was an educated man and had read glowing reports of the novel. Now he read it and realised that it was his daughter's work. He was happy for her to step out of the literary closet and take the plaudits for her creation. When one such message of approval was received from no less a figure than Dr Samuel Johnson, all were delighted.

'Evelina' catapulted Fanny to the forefront of literary society, but it didn't make her rich. Despite its good sales, she made the grand total of £30 from it. However, now established, she received a much healthier figure for her second novel. 'Cecilia, or the Memoirs of an Heiress' earned the young writer £250.

It was also the beginning of the end of her writing career. Or at least the most successful part of it. It is 1786, George III is on the throne, and Caroline is his queen. Bizarre moves were hardly rarities to the mentally suspect king, and he took Fanny into his household, appointing her as 'dresser' to Queen Caroline. Producing novels would interfere with the duties associated with her new role, and this aspect of her writing began to tail off. However, Fanny's journals and letters continued and were published after her death in 1840. They served to provide a fascinating insight into the world of George III's court, as well as her own friendships, especially with Dr Johnson. She married a French refugee, Alexandre D'Arbley, and resided in France until the fall of Napoleon. Once more, Fanny managed to poke a finger into the eye of the establishment. Unusually for the times, as far as we know, their marriage was happy, and unlike many of her counterparts in England, Fanny did not engage in extramarital affairs.

We have seen how Fanny was willing to tackle dangerous subject matters. Her bravery was not limited to the intellectual kind. Incredibly she wrote a first-hand account of her mastectomy. She had the operation in 1810, although we are not sure why. However, she survived and, having endured the operation without anaesthetic, managed to record the experience. Overall, though, her story really is a happy one. Notwithstanding that, she did not manage to gain further literary merit – her last novel was published in 1814 but garnered little enthusiasm from her public. Called 'The Wanderer', it was a work which castigated the insincerity of society. Perhaps this time, it chose a target too loaded; the novel did not run to a second edition. The last thing an insincere person wishes to hear is that she is insincere. An aspect of her life which did continue to thrive, however, was her relationship with her father. The two remained extremely close right up to his death. Not only had she helped him publish his 'History of Music', but she also sent to press three volumes of his memoirs, which she completed in 1832.

Fanny outlived both her husband and son and all three are buried in a family plot in the Regency city of Bath. Hers truly is an uplifting tale.

Although, perhaps, it is hard to say the same about poor Elizabeth Ogilvy Benger. Despite being a lady of fearsome intellect and a great advocate for the influence of women on society, Elizabeth appears to have had a hard life. The reason for this appears to be that, despite her considerable literary skills, she did not have access to the right families or the right connections. As a result, very little is known of her life.

If we are looking for stories of ordinary women who had an influence on Regency Britain and beyond, then Elizabeth Benger seems a fine example to use. Her story, sadly, also illustrates how impoverished a writer's existence could be.

Elizabeth was born in 1778 in Somerset. Her father was a working sailor, and this meant a life on the move as one naval town after another became a temporary home. She was only four when her father was enlisted into the navy, and it seems as though he died in service when she was just eight years old. Equally, none of her siblings survived into adulthood. Although the death of her father left Elizabeth and her mother, Mary, on the borders of destitution, it seems as though Elizabeth had a strong role model in her mother. She encouraged her daughter in her studies, and when the girl displayed a flair for Latin, she even managed to secure her a place in a boys' school (education for girls being, in those days, more of an exercise in etiquette than academia). Elizabeth was just thirteen years old when she penned the poem for which she is perhaps most famous. 'The Female Geniad' is a celebration of the achievements of women over time. It would be, for an educated adult with the realm of literature at their fingertips, a well-researched and superbly crafted piece. For a girl barely in her teens, whose life is dominated by scratching out survival, it is truly incredible.

As she sought to develop her skills, Elizabeth attempted to join the Charles Lamb literary circle but was not accepted into it. Apparently, her adoption of the groups in which the poet, educator and critic Anna Laetitia Aikin (later Barbauld) moved were considered irresolvable to Lamb, and Benger adhered to the more poetic style that her mentor advocated. Lamb carries a reputation as a deep and witty original thinker even today. Maybe though, he was only prepared to think deeply about ideas which fitted neatly within his own prejudices.

Later, as the Regency gained a hold over the cultural mores of the day, Elizabeth published both novels and biographies. These were well received, especially an account of the life of Mary Queen of Scots but did not do enough to cement her a place in the annals of literary history. Indeed, soon after her death, Elizabeth became forgotten. After all, a penniless and childless spinster whose influence over her peers had once been considerable but not long-lasting did not fit neatly into a society for which grandeur was all. On top of that, she was not of the upper class, and since most contemporary recorders of the day were from that limited gene pool, interest in her life and works was inevitably limited.

These days it is hard to find many references to Elizabeth. She appears in 'The Feminist Companion to Literature in English', but even a tome as wide-ranging as the 'Cambridge History of English Literature' offers only a passing mention.[17]

Maybe, though, in some ways, this is a surprise. Elizabeth was a great advocate of women but not politically contentious in promoting her cause. She is the sort of woman who, we might expect, would be welcomed by the establishment. Intelligent and influential but one who also did not actively seek to rock the boat. But she was not 'one of us'. And that accounted for all among the high society leaders of Regency Britain. So Elizabeth became one of the great influencers that never was. A fine writer who barely scraped out an existence; a woman described by Germaine de Stael, the French-Swiss author[18], as the most influential in Britain yet whose reputation flowered while she was alive but quickly withered on her passing.

We can take a lesson from this. In order to become someone in Regency Britain, you must be someone to start with. Only then can your reputation become established. Once more, an example of the elite regenerating itself. Sadly, Elizabeth was not the only one of our writers whose life was marked by struggle.

One of the most prolific writers of this era is Letitia Elizabeth Landon, or L.E.L. as she is better known. L.E.L. was born in 1802 and became a critic of some renown, being the chief reviewer of the Gazette. In this capacity, she held considerable sway over which books became popular and which did not. If our book is partly about those women who held influence and who made a difference, then Letitia certainly deserves her place on these pages.

Her own anthologies were popular and sold well. 'The Fate of Adelaide: A Swiss Tale of Romance; and Other Poems' was her first book, published with the support of her grandmother. This was followed by 'The Improvisatrice; and Other Poems', then the following year, 'The Troubadour: Poetical Sketches of Modern Picture, and Historical Sketches'. These two volumes from 1824 and 1825 marked the high point of her popularity. She followed them with 'The Golden Violet' and 'The Venetian Bracelet' alongside numerous individual works published in everything from gift books to periodicals.

However, with popularity came scrutiny. The feeling among her contemporaries was that L.E.L. overworked herself and suffered mental and physical problems as a result. Like Elizabeth Benger, she did not have access to much, or maybe even anything, in the way of a private income and had to sustain herself through her review work and publishing. Since salaries, especially for women, were low, quantity became necessary even when quality was a given. By 1831 she had moved to the longer form of writing, publishing her first novel 'Romance and Reality'. It was well received, a humorous look at contemporary life. Three further novels will soon follow.

L.E.L. is now confirmed as a leading and highly influential writer of her day. She is a powerful woman… but it does not go down well with those who feel we are pre-ordained to maintain the position into which we are born. Perhaps it is envy; L.E.L. is a successful writer, a woman who has carved out a burgeoning career for herself without a man to support her. A situation which fails to impress society figures. She enjoys the support of forward thinkers such as Lord Byron, but more widely, she becomes subject to speculation about her background and her private life.

Perhaps it is society's expectations which drive her into a relationship with John Forster, who is the editor of the Gazette's rival, The Examiner. Tittle tattle abounds, and Letitia is rumoured to be seeing many other men at the same time.

It speaks of the day, sadly. We do not know the extent, if any, to which Letitia was 'playing the field'. But the assumption is that, as a successful, single woman, she can be doing no other. Behind these libellous conclusions is no more substance than the fact that her family is respectable enough but not of the top drawer. To embark on affairs is acceptable at the time, provided they are discreet. But that seems a rule limited to only the upper classes. At least, that is the perception of that class. Hypocrisy. What else? The relationship with Forster is bound to fail, and it does.

However, in June 1838, Letitia married George Maclean, a Governor in what is now Ghana. It does not appear to be much of a marriage of love. Four months later, L.E.L. commits suicide, taking an overdose of prussic acid.

We are beginning to see a pattern of influence emerge; provided they can break through the morass of convention, our female writers' impact on the literary scene offers inspiration to others and sometimes their sway extends beyond the field of literature. A perfect example of such a person is the Anglo-Irish writer Maria Edgeworth. She was born on New Year's Day of 1768 into an unstable of home. Her parents' marriage was in a regular state of flux, and her mother died when Maria was just six. Her only memory of her mother, it transpires, is of being taken to her bedroom and there given a dying kiss. Beyond that, memories are of her stepmother, who appeared with remarkable rapidity following her biological mother's death. Her parents' marriage really was on the rocks.

Historical novels feature heavily on bestseller lists these days, probably second only to crime books. Many believe that Maria initiated the genre when her novel 'Castle Rackrent' was published in 1800. Set in Ireland, it is possibly also the first truly regional novel in the English language, although Ireland is its setting.

Maria knew Ireland well. Aged fifteen, she travelled there with her family and helped her father manage his estate in the mid-west of the country. Here she gained an insight into the lives of those rural citizens who feature widely in her works. Life is now better than when she was a younger child. It must have been fun and busy. Maria has an astonishing twenty-one siblings – a mixture of step, half and full brothers and sisters. Encouraged but restrained by her father, she begins to write about life around her. The star of her first book, 'The Parent's Assistant', is Rosamund, a lively girl quick to act and slow to think. It has not been since Shakespearean times that real children feature in a work of literature, and although her father forces her to insert some painfully obvious moralising, the work nevertheless sparkles with energy.

Other novels follow. After 'Castle Rackrent' comes 'Belinda', which is slightly marred once more by her father's interference. The happy ending feels artificial, but nevertheless, the book is a success, gaining praise from Jane Austen herself. Ireland continues as her setting as the novels pour forth. Perhaps up there with 'Castle Rackrent' is 'The Absentee', which is included in her six-volume work 'Tales of Fashionable Life'. This powerful piece focuses on the plague of English landowning in Ireland, particularly where the landowner is absent. Maria also writes for children and is perhaps the first author to construct fictional books about real children and their real lives. In a time when childhood among the elite is an artificial experience, her works once more stand high above the writing of her contemporaries. Other influential pieces follow and include 'Patronage' in 1814 and, three years later, 'Ormond'. But 1817 also marks her father's death, and from there, her focus switches more from writing to managing the estate. She does, however, publish her father's memoirs in 1829.

Maria never married, and during the famine of 1846 dedicated her time to supporting starving Irish peasants.

Maria's books stand the test of time well. She was an influence on Sir Walter Scott, amongst others, and is seen as a role model for feminism, a woman who succeeded by herself without the influence of a husband. Her novels remain widely available today.

Another influential Irish writer of the time is Anna Doyle Wheeler (born circa 1780), a highly political and well-travelled writer whose themes include the liberty of women and their education. Anna was another who married into an abusive relationship. She was just fifteen when she was wed into this alcoholic, violent man's household. On the face of it, it must have seemed that the marriage was a wise one. Francis Massey Wheeler was just 19 himself and the son of a Baron. A gentleman in title, yet anything but in behaviour. By the time she turned sixteen, she had her first child, a daughter, and a second was soon on the way. Fortunately, Anna manages to escape her husband's clutches and fled to her uncle's home on the island of Guernsey. However, for the benefit of her daughters, she travels to England and settles in London, there to soon become a part of a circle of social thinkers. As we know, without either a husband or family money (her father was an Irish clergyman), life is tough for a woman alone. Anna, though, is resourceful and manages to scrape out an existence. She works as a translator and also benefits from financial help from friends and family. However, these earnings and donations do not provide enough for a permanent home, and Anna travels around northern Europe to live with friends and relatives. Dublin, Caen and Paris are included among her stops.

In 1830 Anna published 'The Rights of Women' – the title is self-explanatory regarding the content of this important piece. Even more significantly, she becomes a close friend of the social commentator William Thompson. He credits her for many of the ideas in his influential, if awkwardly titled, piece 'Appeal of One Half of the Human Race, Women, Against the Pretensions of the other, Men'.

After the publication of Thompson's work in 1825, Anna's career really takes off. She delivers a lecture on the 'Rights of Women' in London and becomes a part of the controversial but ground-breaking journal 'Tribune Des Femmes'. This French publication was created by working-class women. It promoted the freedom of women and only published works by women. Each, in their way, highly unusual of the time. Even in France.

Unfortunately, by 1840 Anna's health is beginning to deteriorate, and she withdraws from public life. She dies at the age of 63 in 1848.

It was not just in fiction and social commentary that female authors of the Regency made their mark. Maria Edgeworth could well be described as an educator as well as a writer, and the same is true of Jane Marcet.

Marcet, however, wrote about the emerging field of science. Even more, she opened that mysterious world up to women as well as educated white males. Her 1806 work, 'Conversations on Chemistry', was groundbreaking in its conceit. Here the wonders of chemistry are taught to the audience (women, particularly younger ones and girls), but not through the dry, factual account typical of the day. Instead, a teacher talks to two students and answers their questions. The students, though, are not young men from the educated classes. They are women. Such an angle doesn't seem remarkable in any way from today's perspective, but there is no doubt that we can trace the origins of the acceptance of women in science back to the works of Jane Marcet.

Jane was born in 1769, the daughter of wealthy Swiss parents who lived in London. In all likelihood, her education would have included an introduction to science, often referred to as natural philosophy in these days. We can deduce that her fascination for the subject originates there. Her father's business is banking, although we do not have enough details of the family's life to know whether science is a hobby for siblings or parents.

However, in 1799, Jane marries Alexander Marcet, also Swiss, also living in London, but this time a man of medicine. The couple mix in circles which include other scientists and also writers. Alexander practises as a physician, combining this with lecturing at Guys Hospital. Science and education are in the couple's blood. When Jane's father dies in 1817, leaving her a comfortable legacy, her husband chooses to give up work as a doctor and instead concentrates on his study of chemistry.

Jane continued in her love of science, chemistry in particular. However, it seems as though she found some of the concepts difficult, and her husband explained them to her through imaginary conversations between a teacher and a student. That was, apparently, the vogue for the day. Men were considered to be able to absorb information from lectures, whilst the few women whose interests focused on the field of science were generally taught through a question-and-answer technique.

This was her inspiration for 'Conversations on Chemistry' and the numerous 'Conversations on...' books which followed. The teacher in these works is also a lady known as Mrs. B and her students are sisters. The elder, Caroline, asks the questions which lead to the acquisition of understanding, whilst her younger sister, Emily, will ask harder, less expected questions, which take the books down interesting and unpredictable paths. The conceit is clever, encouraging readers to gain a basic understanding whilst also fostering their inquisitiveness.

The books were bestsellers but also academically highly influential. The scientist Michael Faraday was working as a bookbinder's apprentice when he came across the works. He read 'Conversations on Chemistry' and was inspired to pursue a career in science. Just as significant was Jane's vision that science – and the other subjects, such as politics, which she covers in her works – were not just topics for boys. But girls too could, and should, keep apace of changes in these fields.

Each of the writers mentioned above is an influential author of their day. But two, in particular, have carried their reputation into modern times. In fact, for Mary Shelley and Jane Austen, those reputations have, if anything, grown over the decades. That is particularly true of Jane Austen. The writer most of us will think of when the word 'Regency' is mentioned. Nowadays, it is rare to be without a new TV dramatisation of one of her works occupying the prime spot on BBC1 at 9.00pm, a Netflix adaption filling the screens with dodgy accents or a film of one of her works bringing the crowds to the cinema. Her books are a staple of school exam courses and are, of course, still big sellers in major stores and on Amazon. Mary Shelley too. Her 'Frankenstein' is regularly set as a text on GCSE and A Level courses, and the term 'Frankenstein' resonates widely in society. Although, as we will know, the public frequently confuse the 'Dr' with the 'Monster' on this front.

Yet it is Austen's works which have truly captured the imaginations of the nation. Often savagely satirical, her irony more powerful for its gentle but precise targeting, these novels (and their subsequent adaptations) have given us a picture of the Regency period more telling than any museum could ever present.

Jane was born on December 16th, 1775, twenty-two years before Mary Shelley's (nee Wollstonecraft) birth in 1797. She is the second daughter and seventh child of Reverend George Austen and his wife, Cassandra. As the only two daughters among a household of boys (Charles, the youngest, became the sixth brother when he was born), Jane and her elder sister Cassandra are close in age and closer in friendship.

The household is forward-thinking, open and intellectual. The Reverend Austen is also a farmer and a tutor – taking on extra work to feed the growing nest of inquisitive, chirping sparrows he and Mrs Austen continue to produce. The Reverend and Jane become exceptionally close to each other. Indeed, the whole family are tightly bound together – Henry, the fourth brother – will eventually become Jane's literary agent.

Jane and her sister are sent to boarding school at a young age (a fairly common occurrence among the middle classes), and although their father and elder brothers enhanced their learning, this is not enough for a girl greedy for knowledge, so Jane reads widely on her own. It is a truth that books inspire a love of literature. Although money is never particularly abundant in the household, the home contains a library and a wide collection of literature which Jane and Cassandra are encouraged to use. The Reverend Austen motivates his daughters' creativity with a ready supply of writing equipment.

Theirs is a happy household, one which abounds with humour and good-natured debate. The family love nothing more than to devise and improvise plays, write scripts and act out their creations. It is possible to see quite easily how such a lively imagination as Jane's is encouraged. She delves into experimentation with different forms of literature, writing plays, poems and even a book of letters. Unusually for the time, hers is a home where it is fine to fail, to be original and to challenge convention. Despite those different genres in which she experimented, it is, of course, for her novels that we remember her best.

Jane was in her early twenties when in 1797, Mary Wollstonecraft Godwin, later Shelley, was born. If her literary peer grew up in a home of gay abandon in the beautiful, open Hampshire countryside (her father's parish was the village of Steventon), then Mary's upbringing was decidedly different. There was none of the fun and freedom of the

Austen household. Mary's father was the philosopher William Godwin, whose political writings were famed among the intellectual classes; her mother was also well known, the active feminist Mary Wollstonecraft. One can imagine a home of intensity, of debate, true, but while the Austen household argued with humour and fun, the Godwins would be earnest and serious. Although, if that was indeed the case, young Mary would understand little of it. Her mother died when she was still a baby, leaving William to care for her and her half-sister Fanny (the result of an affair between her mother and a soldier).

Another Mary entered the family when our Mary was just four years old. Mary Jane Clairmont became her stepmother when she married William Godwin in 1801, and the relationship between these two Marys was strained. The family grew as Clairmont brought in her own two children and, together with Godwin, produced another child – a son. This mixed bag of siblings of differing degrees of biological proximity never gelled, and it did not help when Clairmont decided that her own biological daughter should be educated, but not Mary.

However, it does seem that her relationship with her father was close, even if he was distracted by his work. He published a poem she wrote aged ten – 'Mounseer Nongtonpaw' and, just as with Jane Austen fifty miles and twenty years away in Hampshire, allowed his daughter free access to his jam-packed library. If that were not enough to inspire his daughter and her love of literature, guests at the house included the great poets Wordsworth and Coleridge. 'As a child,' she wrote, 'I scribbled; and my favourite pastime, during the hours given me for recreation, was to write stories.'[19]

Jane Austen's books feature thwarted or difficult-to-achieve romance. A question scholars pose is often around the extent to which these books are a reflection of her own life. Jane never married, although most likely would have done, had it not been for the power of families to intervene when they decided that a prospective wife offered insufficient funds to deserve their son's love.

In or around 1795, the nephew of one of Jane's neighbours began to visit Steventon on a regular basis. The purpose of these visits was, it seems, to see Jane. This was Tom Lefroy, a young man studying in London and planning to enter the profession of law. Jane later wrote that she and Tom had fallen in love, and she regularly wrote to Cassandra regarding this burgeoning romance.

But Lefroy was being sponsored in his studies by family members, and they clearly thought a Reverend's daughter from a tiny Hampshire village an unsuitable wife for their young relative. Particularly one who engaged in such airy-fairy nonsense as writing. The Reverend Austen certainly could not provide a dowry, and so Lefroy's family ended the relationship. Had it been twenty years later, then, in all likelihood, the changes brought about by the Regency would have prevented this, allowing Jane and Tom to follow their hearts. Although whether Jane would still have presented the world with such classics as 'Mansfield Park' or 'Pride and Prejudice' had she finally satisfied her own romantic desires can only be a matter of speculation.

Mary Shelley's love interest, though, was satisfied (of sorts), albeit some twenty years later, in the middle of the Regency. By then, she was a changed person. In 1812 she had experienced something of which she had previously held no true concept. A home full of domestic bliss. Like that of the Austens. She had gone to stay with a friend of her father, William Baxter, and his family. The household in Scotland gave her an insight into happiness she had not felt before, and she returned the following year. Her outlook was changed, and in 1814 she began to fall in love with another poet who was a regular visitor to her London home. Percy Bysshe Shelley was an acolyte of her father. A man he regarded as a mentor and advisor for his own creations. Soon, though, his attentions turned to the daughter. Percy Shelley was older and already married. Still, that did not stop him from absconding from England. Accompanied, controversially, by his teenage love. Both partners' relationship with Godwin was damaged, but their love could prosper away from the stifling London home.

This was unlike the Shelleys' financial fortunes. Struggling for money, domestic tragedy also struck the couple. As they travelled through Europe, their baby was born, but the girl died soon after birth. The following year, Mary's half-sister, Fanny, committed suicide, and then Shelley's abandoned wife followed suit. The tragedy allowed Mary and Percy to marry, which they did at the end of 1816.

The previous year, though, the couple had stayed in Switzerland with Lord Byron and some friends. It was during a rain-filled day that the group had read ghost stories to each other, and Byron suggested they each write their own.

That was the genesis of Mary Shelley's greatest and most famous work. 'Frankenstein, or the Modern Prometheus'. It was not, however, Mary's first published piece. In 1817 she published a travelogue of their European adventures, called 'History of a Six Weeks' Tour'. The following year 'Frankenstein, or the Modern Prometheus' hit the world. Published anonymously, the novel was a roaring success. Despite the anonymity of its author, the thinking was that Percy Bysshe Shelley had penned the work. After all, he had written the introduction to it. Perhaps it is indicative of the times that nobody believed it could be his wife who had created such a masterpiece.

The relationship between the poet and the novelist did not easily fit into a category. Adultery plagued them, and two more children died young. In fact, only their son Percy Florence survived. Then, in 1822, Percy drowned in a sailing accident. He was just thirty. Mary a mere twenty-four. As is no surprise, life for a woman without a husband was hard. There was little support from her husband's family – his father disapproved of his son's lifestyle. Although it is 'Frankenstein' that we associate with Mary, after her husband's death, she wrote several more novels, including 'Valperga' and 'The Last Man'. She also committed herself to the promotion of Percy's poetry. She died of brain cancer in 1851, living back in the city of her birth, London. Her last book to be published, 'Mathilde' did not see the light of day until around a century after her own death, when it was released in the 1950s.

Jane Austen, meanwhile, continued to work on her own literary career. Her father helped all that he could, at one point trying to get one of her works published through Thomas Cadell. Cadell, apparently, did not even open the manuscript. There stood a man blessed with foresight. Meanwhile, the books which would come to be known as 'Pride and Prejudice' and 'Northanger Abbey' were taking shape.

Provisionally titled 'First Impressions' and 'Susan', respectively, each went through many drafts and substantial revisions.

Then, as the new century dawned, Reverend Austen announced that he was to retire, a piece of news which seemed a shock to all. It meant, of course, that they would need to give up the Rectory, and indeed the whole family moved to Bath. Jane was sad to leave the idyll of Steventon and her childhood home.

It was while living in Bath that Jane came closest to marriage. Harris Bigg-Wither is not some character from Dickens but a real person (presumably one whose parents either had a sense of humour or absolutely none). Bigg-Wither was due to inherit a Bigg-Wither of a family fortune and was attracted to Jane. The arrangements seemed suitable. Jane would marry, enjoy financial stability and becomes a good wife to her husband, although such a surname might not do much for a serious writer's fledgling career.

There was only one matter missing from the arrangement. A fairly crucial one. It seemed that Jane felt no affection for the man urging her to become his wife. Having accepted his proposal, the next day, she rejected it. A woman whose creations would only marry for love, not for financial gain or social standing, acted true to the spirit of those characters. Who has not been inspired by an Elizabeth Bennett or Mary Crawford? As she said to a member of her family many years later, 'Marry for love but nothing else.'[20]

In January 1805, George Austen died. This close family was thrown into turmoil by the tragedy. There was little money, but the brothers agreed to look after their mother and sisters. Doing so meant much moving about and at times hardship. But they stuck together. The effect on Jane was to bring a halt to her writing. In the circumstances in which she was now living, creativity seemed to have left her.

Then, Jane, her mother and Cassandra were offered a permanent home by their brother Edward. Chawton Cottage provided the setting and security to send Jane once more off on a creative streak. Her novel, 'Susan', lay in the hands of a tardy, and possibly double-crossing, publisher called Mr Crosby. He tries to con Jane out of £10 – a fortune to a woman without financial means – in order to sort of vanity publish the work. She refuses. Such is her financial situation that she could do nothing else even if she wished to. But Jane is able to write once more and recognising this, her family allow her to work and take on her share of the household jobs in order to let her do so. Particularly supportive is her brother Henry who, while pursuing his own career in banking, takes on the responsibility of becoming her literary agent. He approaches Thomas Egerton, a publisher based in London, and he is the one who finally sees the genius that is Jane Austen. He publishes 'Sense and Sensibility' in 1811, and on the tide of the Regency Act, the book sells out quickly, despite little in the way of marketing or publicity.

Then, in January 1813, he is presented with 'Pride and Prejudice', and he knows he has another winner on his hands. This time the novel is promoted and marketed widely, and its initial run sells out within months. Next comes 'Mansfield Park'. Jane is still publishing her works anonymously, and this is not uncommon at the time. In fact, they will not be attributed to Jane during her lifetime. Her modesty seems to be another virtue she has acquired from her loving family. A characteristic, perhaps, in which some of the well-known in London might have usefully invested. Among the snootier literati, the notion of a (probable – we do not know if they were aware of the writer's name) woman, one from the sticks at that, taking the publishing world by storm is the literary equivalent of a hay fever sufferer falling asleep in a meadow. They awake snorting and sniffling and generally trying to do down this upstart writer. But the public has discovered their Austen, and once more, this latest novel sells quickly, actually becoming Egerton's most profitable publication. The money which subsequently makes its way to the Austen family is welcome but not substantial given the finances the works generate, and Jane decides to find a new publisher. This will be one of the leading publishing houses of its day, that of John Murray. (In fact, it seems as though Jane earns in the region of £600 to £650 during her life; the equivalent of around £70000-£80000 today. Not a sum to be sneezed at but hardly of John Grisham proportions.)

It is under John Murray that 'Emma', 'Northanger Abbey' and 'Persuasion' are published, along with a further edition of 'Mansfield Park'. The Austen family, though, are suffering financial hardship once more, with Henry's banking career having imploded and investments lost. Jane's health, too, is beginning to deteriorate. The Regency period is at its flamboyant height in 1816, and its greatest writer and, arguably, most famous child is struggling. But Jane is used to hard work. She finishes one book, 'The Elliots' and starts another. By April 1817, her health had deteriorated so much, though, that she was confined to her bed. She died on July 18th, 1817, and, thanks to

Henry and his connections, is buried in Winchester Cathedral. Now is the time that Henry releases his sister's name to the world, and six of the greatest works of not just the Regency period but perhaps throughout the whole of literature can be attributed to their proper author. Jane Austen. A fairly ordinary woman with a remarkably close and loving family. A woman of great inner strength and, like her sister, brothers and parents, huge generosity who just happens to be able to pen stories that capture people's hearts. Stories of love which, other than for one brief period, elude their creator.

CHAPTER 5

ALL THE WORLD'S A STAGE: ACTRESSES AND ARTISTES

To be a writer is frowned upon during Regency times and those around it. To be an actress is even more poorly regarded. Other than for the very, very elite, it is to live at best a disreputable life, at worst to exist as barely more than a prostitute. If one does not quite sell her body to the paying public, then she sells her character. Often, as a disreputable one, given the presentation of women in contemporary drama. Although maybe one person altered that perception.

If proof were needed that a woman from the Regency period, other than Jane Austen, can continue to carry prominence, then it can be found in Sarah Siddons. Siddons was, without too much doubt, the most renowned actress not only of the Regency period but perhaps of the entire eighteenth and nineteenth centuries. Her name continues today as a torchbearer for the importance of theatre. Not just London, either. For example, the Sarah Siddons Society provides scholarships for budding young performers in the Chicago area, and the Sarah Siddons Fan Club celebrates the strange and macabre, through drama and promenades, in Southampton. On Paddington Green, London, a statue based on Reynolds' 1784 painting 'Mrs. Siddons as the Tragic Muse' dominates the small park. It carries sufficient importance for her nose, broken by some act, to be replaced in 2019. Her statue was just the second to be erected in London, which represented an actor. Its only predecessor being one of Shakespeare.

Sarah was committed to her career. Astonishingly so. She even gave birth – literally – to one of her children during a performance. In a pattern we will see repeated throughout this chapter, Sarah was born in 1775 into a family of thespians. These were the Kembles – more of whom later. In fact, her future husband joined her in her father's troupe – that was William Siddons, and they were married in 1773, from whence she became known as Mrs Siddons. Although, for a woman who would later command audiences so absolutely that the term 'Siddonimania' was used to describe the effect she had on theatregoers, her London debut was not the greatest of successes. Indeed, she described herself as 'banished from Drury Lane as a worthless candidate for fame and fortune.'[21] After debuting at Drury Lane, a couple of years after marrying William, she returned to regional theatre, becoming a star of the Theatre Royal, Bath. Seven years after her inauspicious start to life treading the London boards, she returned (in 1782), performing under the wings of the great actor Irving, who had introduced her to London audiences. Her role was the eponymous lead in Hamilton's 'The Tragedy of Isabella'… and she wowed the London crowd.

It was, however, as Lady Macbeth that Sarah found her most lasting success and her greatest performances. It certainly helped that she looked the part. Lady Macbeth's power in the early acts of Shakespeare's tragedy makes her downfall so mighty. Sarah was tall and beautiful and held her own kind of natural dignity. Perfect for the role.

Maybe her husband should have taken heed of the fact she refused to cancel a performance for the somewhat demanding activity of giving birth. Such was her commitment to acting (after several years as the leading lady of Drury Lane, she moved across the street to Covent Garden) that her marriage took second place. Maybe this contributed to the fact that of her seven children, only two were still alive when she herself died in 1831.

Her final performance came on June 29th, 1812, with the fifty-seven-year-old actress once more reprising her greatest role. The story is that such was the clamour for her finale that the play had to be abandoned after her scene in Act V, where Lady Macbeth appears for the last time. That sleepwalking scene is, of course, one of Shakespeare's most powerful and most famous. The curtains closed after it, only reopening after a long pause to reveal Sarah Siddons as herself. Apparently, she then gave an impromptu speech which continued for ten minutes, her awe-inspired audience as mesmerised as during her greatest performances.

Like the best of those who love the limelight, retirement was only temporary, and she returned to the stage for a number of performances and readings over the ensuing years, right up until her death. By then, she was renowned as the greatest actress in the history of theatre, and more than five thousand people lined the streets for her funeral.

Even if no other actress during that period could quite match the reputation and acclaim of Sarah Siddons, several others became notable figures of their day. Included amongst these must be the Viennese actress cum singer Maria Therese Du Camp. Not only was she born (in 1774 – she died in 1838) into a theatrical family, but she would later become the sister-in-law of Sarah Siddons, marrying her brother, Charles. (From which point on, she took the name Maria Kemble.)

Maria was brought to England soon after she was born, making her debut at the Opera House when she was just six years old. By age twelve, she had performed in front of the royal family. The kind of single-minded determination we see in Sarah Siddons was present in Maria also. Her father returned to Germany while she was still a child and died there soon after. She taught herself English and was determined to make a name for herself. After marrying Charles, she worked for much of the remainder of her career at the Covent Garden, where she played supporting roles to her husband's leading parts.

Maria was a well-regarded actress. She regularly features in the newspapers of the days, advertising her performances. These include the London papers, such as the Daily Post but also ones from the provinces – Bath, Leicester, Bristol and Hull are just four examples. Indeed, the Hull Advertiser proudly tells in, in 1809, that she will appear for six nights in a production of the comedy 'Belle's Strategem'. 'Mrs C Kemble – Six Nights' reads the heading. The report goes on to say, 'From the Theatre Royal, Drury Lane and the Hay-Market – Her first appearance on this (the Hull) stage.'

While Sarah Siddons and Maria Kemble enjoyed successful careers and earned the adoration of audiences, we must not forget that for many, a career on stage was considered potentially dishonourable and could be regarded, at worst, as a form of prostitution. High-class prostitution often involving the satisfaction of urges from men of family and stature but disreputable nonetheless. Such were the circumstances in which a young actress called Maria Foote found herself. In her case, as we shall see, it seems as though even her father was happy to see her passed between men of means. Provided, that is, it benefitted him.

Maria was born around the turn of the 1800s into a family of thespians. Her father ran a theatre in Plymouth, and by her late teens, she had performed not only there but also in Paris. It appears as though the young Maria may not have been the finest actor but was blessed with stunning good looks. There were more ways than one to keep the male portion of an audience entertained in those days.

She was performing at Cheltenham when she caught the eye of one Colonel, William Fitzhardinge Berkeley. He happened to be the eldest son of the Earl of Berkeley and had a reputation as a playboy and, to use an old-fashioned term, complete cad. However, maybe he was genuine when offering to support her benefit, which was a kind of one-off performance at which the actor might receive the takings. Probably, though, he wasn't. The Colonel's life was embroiled in controversy. He was attempting to secure his own inheritance of his father's Earldom after some shenanigans over his parents' marriage. He was also a failed politician, having been given a Gloucestershire parliamentary seat in 1810 only to lose it a year later.

But, whatever, he and the teenage Maria soon became lovers. At least we must presume they did since she gave birth to two children. The official story tells a different story, however. It claims that she remained living with her parents, by now in London, and the Colonel never 'stayed over'. The Colonel, however, refused to marry his young mistress and make the relationship official. In fact, following each birth, he insisted that Maria and the children retire to the country – ostensibly for their own protection but, in reality, to keep the additions to his family secret. Theirs was an affair of the times, publicly deplored but privately accepted, provided it was kept discreet. Of course, by being sent to the country, Maria was forced to pause her own growing career on the stage.

It was while she was pregnant with their second child that Joseph Hayne made an entrance. The son of a wealthy plantation owner, Hayne had been born in the Caribbean, but his family-owned land in Staffordshire. As was the way with this romantic era, Hayne had seen his muse on stage and fallen madly in love. He was a man used to getting his way. He invited Samuel Foote, Maria's father and supposed keeper of morals, to his pile in Staffordshire in order to further his opportunities with the attractive young actress. Samuel was happy to oblige, telling the landowner that his daughter was currently illicitly bound to the Colonel, but once that passed on, he was welcome to make his move.

Hayne, though smitten and entitled, was at least a man of some honour. Following Maria's return to London after the birth of her second child, she finally realised that the Colonel had zero intention of doing the honourable thing and ended their relationship. Hayne stepped in immediately, making an offer of marriage. News quickly reached Berkeley, who, it is believed, found the whole thing highly amusing. After all, what is the loss of one mistress when you have plenty of others?

He ensured Hayne found out about the babies and suggested that Maria should choose between the two. Once more, Hayne acted with some honour, immediately breaking off his engagement to the unfortunate Maria, who must have felt like a ship being tossed between two great rocks: one cold and immovable, the other eroding with each hit. Berkeley announced he was going to 'console' Maria, in the process giving Hayne the derogatory nickname, 'Pea Green'.

If the story already sounds as convoluted as a Regency comedy, we have only seen Act 1. The marriage to Hayne is now off, then it is on again before it runs through a repeat of the same farce at least a couple more times. Including, on one occasion, Hayne alleging that he was made drunk by his friends, who locked him in a room to prevent him from attending the wedding. Of course, Samuel Foote is meanwhile very keen on his daughter's matrimony taking place. The considerable sum of £40000 has been settled on the wedding, and he is anxious to get his hands on the cash.

It does now seem as though Hayne is genuinely having second thoughts, and his previously honourable behaviour starts to go on the turn. Apparently, Haynes, perhaps egged on by his friends, thinks that there might be some money to be had for a breach of promise if he can just prove that he knew nothing of his maybe fiancée's relationship with Colonel Berkeley. The complex plot thickens. He seeks 'to put the Public in possession of facts' which, in his own words, '...will justify my conduct' as he so nobly puts it in a letter to the Morning Post, which was published on October 16th, 1824.[22]

As for our tragic heroine Maria, she faces ruin. She has committed to marrying Hayne, a man she has not only loved as much as Berkeley but, as it turns out, just as naively. To fulfil her promise, she has curtailed her career, sent her cupboard of costumes to be sold, and paid for a carriage to take her, in full matrimonial glory, to her wedding. Now the pretty worm turns herself, and she decides to sue Hayne for his own breach of promise, and indeed wins her case. But only as a woman might in a man's world. The compensation she receives is small.

Fortunately, in true Regency fashion, the final scene of the story ends happily. Maria restarts her career on stage, and the publicity surrounding her experiences makes her even more popular than before. Soon, she finds true and proper love, marrying Charles Stanhope, the Viscount Petersham. Together they have a family of their own. Applause, bow and curtain down.

Liaisons with the rich and famous seemed to haunt actresses of the Regency period. Dorothea Jordan's career may well be a fine example of it not being what you can do, but who you know that enables you to make your name. Dorothea (1761-1816) – sometimes known as Dorothy – comes from humble stock. Her mother was an actress. Not though, an especially well-known one. Grace Phillips performed on the Dublin stage and married a stagehand. It is, therefore, not a surprise that young Dorothea would follow her parents into the life of a thespian. She made her debut, also in Dublin, when she was just fifteen, playing Shakespeare's Phoebe in 'As You Like It'. What is far more surprising is that her portrait can still be seen in the National Portrait Gallery. She would, in time, become the subject of such important artists as Gainsborough, Romney and Reynolds.

But there was little in her early career to suggest that she would gain such fame and prominence. Indeed, Dorothea leaves Dublin sometime around 1780, still a teenager, and works with a provincial theatre company, Tate Wilkinson, for the next five years. The likelihood is that Dorothea is a good actress. She specialises in comedy roles, and in particular those of a rough and ready, Tomboy-type character. Further, Tate Wilkinson is a well-respected company run by the eponymous actor who had enjoyed a successful career of his own on stage, despite the trickiness in those days of satirising figures of note.

Tate Wilkinson would eventually take over the York theatre circuit, with productions appearing throughout the North, taking in York, Newcastle, Beverley and Hull before, later, extending to such conurbations as Hull, Leeds and Wakefield. So, Dorothea became a part of the company, but it was not this which led her to the walls of the National Portrait Gallery. In fact, no less than 29 portraits, in various forms, exist of her.

It was after she left Tate Wilkinson and began to appear on the London stage that her career really began to flourish. Dorothea gained the reputation as London's leading comic actress.

She never married but called herself Mrs Jordan. Respectability being all. In fact, Dorothea gave birth to five children – including one with her first stage manager in Ireland – before finding the love of her life. A man whom, given her own humble beginnings, she could not marry.

It is through her work that she comes to the attention of a significant member of the aristocracy. The Duke of Clarence, no less, the third son of George III and a man who will, in time, ascend to the throne as King William IV. The duke already has a reputation as proliferate; he is constantly short of money and uses his position as a senior royal to enjoy a wild life. Certainly, for a comic actress with a growing reputation, entering into an affair with the King's son is no bad thing for her career. But the relationship is genuinely about more than this. Over a twenty-year period, beginning in 1790, there will be no less than ten children, and it seems a close and loving relationship. But the Duke is a habitual spender – it seems to run in the family. Even after his father has presented him with Bushey House and estate just outside North London, the Duke frequently remains short of funds, and even as a high-ranking royal relies heavily on Dorothea, a member of that disreputable clan known as 'actresses', to supplement his income from her own earnings.

Unusually, their affair is a public one, although it is still officially frowned upon whilst privately accepted. It is that kind of period. And also, the kind of times where, when something more pressing emerges, it is the woman who is pushed to the wayside. In 1811 the Regency officially begins, and the powers that be recognise that, however unlikely, the possibility now exists that William might become King.

Certainly, Frederick and the Regent, George himself, are higher in the line of ascendency, but these are uncertain times.

The Royal Family decides that appearances must take precedence over love. The duke is instructed to abandon his affair and find a wife. (He eventually married Adelaide of Saxe-Meinegan in 1818.) Further, that wife must meet two criteria. She must be royal, and she must be rich.

It is easy to see Dorothea as promiscuous and somebody who placed her own career above all else. After all, she was an actress famed for portraying bawdy roles on the London stage, albeit playing them extremely well. She had fifteen children from at least three different men. She never married but adopted the title Mrs. The veil of respectability being all.

Such assumptions are easily made, but the truth is far more complex. She used her own earnings to purchase Gifford Lodge on Twickenham Green. The splendid home was used to provide a good upbringing for those children who were not fathered by the duke. Meanwhile, she was supporting the duke financially and was clearly happy in their relationship. Indeed, when it was ended by pressure from the Royal Family, she was apparently devastated. The duke attempted to do the right thing and granted her a generous settlement to share with her family, which consisted of, of course, in part his own children.

Sadly, shortly after her retirement as an actress, she was betrayed by her own son-in-law, who ran up enormous debts in her name. Shamed and penniless, she crossed the Channel and died in absolute poverty.

Although, some rumours exist that, in fact, she returned secretly to England and lived on privately for many years. Proof of this has never come to light. It would be nice, though, if it were, in fact, true.

As for the Duke, he became king in 1831, following the death of brother Frederick in 1827 and George IV himself in 1830. One of his first decisions was to order a statue of his mistress to be sculpted. His love for Dorothea never going away.

Tate Wilkinson also played a substantial role in the career of another leading actress of her day. Like Dorothea, Maria Duncan Davison (circa 1780-1858) came from theatrical stock. Not much is known about her parents, other than they were actors who most probably worked in the Liverpool area, and similarly, not much is known about the young Maria. However, she was almost certainly a child actress and one who appeared across the north of these islands, travelling as far west as Dublin and up to Edinburgh on occasion.

Maria had a love for the Scottish city, and indeed this is why she eventually abandoned a flourishing career in London. This had begun following a highly successful run in Margate in 1804 when she was tempted by the part of Lady Teazle in Richard Brinley Sheridan's 'The School for Scandal'. She accepted the role and spent fourteen years with the theatre company playing the leading lady in hit after hit. She created the role of Juliana in John Tobin's comedy 'The Honeymoon'. Her performance drew the following comment from a prominent critic of the day 'Her acting during the dance with Lopez is the finest piece of pantomime the stage has ever seen.'[23]

Another whose association with the stage led to fortune, if not especially fame, was Harriot Mellon. Like the others mentioned already, she was born into a theatrical family. That was in 1777 or thereabouts. In fact, her father was the wardrobe keeper of a company of touring actors. In such circumstances, it is not surprising that she found herself onstage, making her debut at the age of just ten. However, it was when she was spotted by Irish playwright and long-time owner of Drury Lane Theatre Richard Sheridan that matters really took off. The author of such plays as 'The Rivals' saw in Harriot both talent and good looks, and he employed her for a season at his theatre.

There was another characteristic which Harriot held in abundance – a good nature. It was this and its attendant lack of driving ambition that enabled her to enjoy a career understudying for the leading actresses of the day. These included both Sarah Siddons and Dorothea Jordan. She also took on comic roles of her own.

Then, in 1815, she married Thomas Coutts, of Coutts Bank fame. She was not especially welcomed into the family by his three children from his first wife, but that did not stop her looking after them after Thomas died, just seven years into their marriage. It was at this point that Harriet displayed another, less well published, skill. Business. She became a key operator and decision maker at Coutts, working as the active senior partner who held half the shares in the bank. At the same time, she granted her three stepdaughters an annual stipend of £10,000 and ensured her step-grandchildren would inherit her share of the business in time.

She did remarry. Unusually, for the time, to a younger man, the 9th Duke of St Albans who enjoyed the unwieldy moniker of William Aubrey de Vere Beauclerk. After her death, she granted him a substantial annual income and use of two of her homes, but the majority of her fortune, worth close to £2 million, was left to her step-granddaughter, Angela Burdett. The inheritance came with stipulations but nevertheless was a sign of her loyalty to her first husband. Maria's life is notable not only for her success both as an actress and a businesswoman. Being the daughter of a travelling wardrobe master really casts her as being from working-class stock, albeit upper working class. Yet to be the chief shareholder of a bank as important as Coutts is a role reserved for the upper classes. Maria proved that, with talent, determination, good fortune and perhaps a character which made few enemies, it was possible to move through the hardened ceilings of the Regency class system. Maybe the changes in attitudes of the Regency, to which we have alluded earlier, were responsible for the tiny cracks in those ceilings which made movement possible... if still, extremely unusual.

So, what might we deduce from this brief look at actresses from the Regency period? It seems as though a sound upbringing in the arts is an important precursor to a successful career on the stage. Perhaps these fledgling careers were helped, in the strangest of ways, by the very conventions which acted on those with the greatest chance of becoming successful. The upper classes. Those pressures were the very opposites of the sort of characteristics an actress would need to possess, and as such, there was little competition from the most entitled members of society. Undoubtedly, had it been different, these were the women who would have been given the best opportunities to succeed. The juiciest roles. But maybe it is also true that to play a part effectively, you have to know a little more about real life than a lady brought up with every advantage (bar her gender) might experience.

Upon reaching London, actresses became the object of attention for many a member of the gentry and aristocracy. Cynically, we might conclude that the reputation with which their profession was imbued made them, in the eyes of predatory men, fair game. Sometimes, though, even that worked out for the good. More often, it did not. For every Sarah Siddon or Dorothea Jordan, many more provincial actresses never found fame. Never made their fortune and indeed scraped a living from travelling from town to City, forever on the move.

And while the most famous became figures of adoration, for most, the career was considered disreputable at best and often salacious. But, of course, the stories of these actresses' lives have not been recorded. We can only guess at the hardships they endured.

CHAPTER 6

MAKING A DIFFERENCE

We know that the spring smell of change is sweetening the air. The old ways are under threat, and a move towards some degree of equality is illuminating the lives of the downtrodden. But that change is snail-like. Women still suffer from a lack of available education. Even those with access to this follow a curriculum very different from that of boys. The expectations on women to behave in a certain way – still subordinate even if less so than in previous eras – remain suffocating, and conventions limit their opportunities for self-expression. Sitting like a storm-charged cloud above all that hangs the all-pervading threats of the class system, ready to pour down on any who seek to improve their chances. Still, not all remain suppressed. We have looked at women who changed lives through their literature and through their performances on the stage. But many others make a difference through their expertise, commitment and determination in other fields. Their names may not be quite as well known today as Jane Austen, Mary Shelley or Sarah Siddons, but their influence is certainly great, speeding up that slow process towards greater, if still diminished, opportunity.

The fields of the women we will now look towards are varied. There are women from business, from science, and those who are leading social reformers. These are women from all strata of society. From one who shared a home with the Prime Minister of Britain to others from the emerging middle classes and even one who inhabited an impoverished part of Regency life. Each, though, played their part in making Britain a fairer, more educated, more prosperous place. For all.

We touched on the conditions facing women in prison in our introduction. Women were found to be in need of rehabilitation not just once but twice. Firstly, the woman's criminality must be addressed. Punishment and retraining followed, often including isolation for months on end. While men endured hard labour, it is true that often women did not, but their own form of torture was a mental one. Even that was not considered enough. A woman who transgresses requires not only retribution for her crime but must offer further penance. This time for her felony against womanhood. Or man's perception of this, to be more precise.

Even today, two hundred years on, there is a widely held belief that the only way to treat prisoners is to punish them. That, somehow, to treat a criminal well and help them reintegrate into society through proper education and civilised care is soft and an insult to law-abiding people. After two hundred years of reform, prisons are often falling apart, dirty, smelly, unsanitary and desperately over-crowded. Imagine, then, what conditions were like for detainees in 1813.

This is the year in which Elizabeth Fry visits Newgate prison in London. What this quaker and social reformer sees appals her. She is sickened by the filth, the desperate conditions, and the inhumanity facing women and children. Unsurprisingly, mental illness is rife, unchecked and untreated. She resolves, there and then, to do something about it because Elizabeth Fry is that kind of woman.

Elizabeth was born in 1780 into a large family. She has six siblings, and although comfortably off, her early childhood is not particularly happy. She is a quiet child, and her brothers and sisters loud. Elizabeth is afraid of the dark and small, enclosed spaces. Childhood games such as hide and seek terrify, rather than entertain, her. Perhaps it is that fear which will later enable her to empathise with prisoners squeezed into cramped, dangerous corners with inadequate supervision and a lack of basic facilities.

The adult forms out of the child, and as a young woman, Elizabeth remains socially isolated, plagued by fears. Timid. Something which is not what we would expect given the evidence of the lady she became. Her Quaker upbringing also defines her, and the teachings of that religion regarding the importance of supporting the poor are a major influence on her life. Yet, for all her good deeds and intentions, she is a woman who is unsure of her place in the world, and so it is her religion on which she increasingly leans as she seeks a purpose for her existence. She marries Joseph Fry, a fellow Quaker, in 1800 but still is plagued by the notion that she has a calling, she just does not know yet what it is.

During a Quaker meeting, a visitor from America stands and speaks. It is William Savery, a preacher, and his words are magnetic to the young Elizabeth. He urges the gathering to be thankful for the life they have been given and use that as a starting point to do good. Elizabeth is inspired. Already committed to their plight, she dedicates herself to the poor. She decides it is time to take the lead and not just react to what is around her. She realises that giving food or money to the poor is important, of course, but it is a deed which helps just the recipient. But to really make a difference, she must tackle the circumstances under which the poor live.

It is with zeal that she visits Newgate and is appalled by the hell she witnesses. Men, women, and children crowded together. Desperate, violent criminals housed with people guilty of no more than stealing an apple or a loaf of bread. Often guilty of no more than their poverty or of having a parent, rather than themselves, convicted.

Elizabeth acts immediately, gathering together her wealthy friends and sewing clothes for the inmates, baking bread which she delivers the next day. She organises a school for the children of the prison. How else to break the pattern of innocence growing into criminality than through education? She teaches the children herself. She fights for the segregation of male and female prisoners, with female matrons to oversee the incarcerated women. Education spreads out from, initially, the prison's children to include women. Constructive work (knitting, sewing) is brought in to make productive use of what was previously monotony. An occupied mind is a happier, calmer, more purposeful mind. Mental health improves just a little, and with it, behaviour. Word spreads, and people begin to take notice.

But it takes time. Four years after that first visit to Newgate prison, Elizabeth forms the Association for the Improvement of Female Prisoners and, together with a dozen of her peers, lobbies for change. She persuades Parliament that improving conditions will bring about an improvement in outcomes. Not just for the prisoners but for the society to which most will eventually return. It still takes more time, but in 1823, ten years after she first stepped through the gates of Newgate prison, Parliament finally introduces legislation for reform.

It was not just prison to which Elizabeth turned her benevolent but determined eyes. Mental asylums were no more than prisons where all, rather than just some, suffered debilitating emotional illness. They, too, were ripe for reform. She fought for twenty-five years to improve the convict ship system, visiting every ship that left for Australia before it set sail. She did not limit her attention to the criminal or mentally ill underclasses. She fought for education for all women, for improvements in housing, and was behind the concept of the soup kitchen to support the poorest members of society.

Elizabeth died in 1845, having made a difference. A big one. A friend by now of Queen Victoria, a decision was made that something must be created to be a more recognisable legacy to all that she achieved for the poor. The Lord Mayor of London led the drive for this, and the Elizabeth Fry Refuge was formed. This was to be an institute to support ex-prisoners. That legacy continues today in the form of the Elizabeth Fry Charity, which runs an official hostel for women.

Elizabeth Fry epitomises those women of the period who demonstrated that they could make a difference in all walks of life.

Another whose work remains very notably commemorated today is Marie Tussaud.

Marie Tussaud was born in 1761 and never knew her father. He was killed in the Seven Years' War a couple of months before she was born. The death had a significant impact on her future life. With no husband, her mother, Anne-Marie Walder, travelled to Bern in Switzerland. There she was employed as a housekeeper by Dr Philippe Curtius. Dr Curtius became a significant figure in Marie's life. She grew close enough to him to call the Doctor 'uncle'. It was his job, however, for which we should be grateful (or not, if we have queued for half a day on the Marylebone Road hoping to see one of the country's foremost tourist destinations). Dr Philippe Curtius was a physician but also a sculptor. His specialism was to construct anatomical models from wax. Later, he produced portraits as well. When the good doctor moved to Paris to pursue his artistic career, Anne-Marie and Marie soon followed. In the child, Dr Curtius had found a good student, and that student, in turn, had an excellent teacher. Together, they shared a relationship close enough for the two to care about each other but not quite as close as the sort of parent/child relationship, which can make learning difficult.

The Doctor was also a fine sculptor. Good enough to be commissioned to produce a model of Louis XV's mistress, Madame Du Barry, and also prolific enough to hold two Paris exhibitions, the second being a precursor to the Chamber of Horrors, which is these days a staple of any waxworks and is the biggest attraction at Madam Tussauds. By her middle teens, Marie Tussaud was producing outstanding waxworks of her own. Voltaire, Franklin. Even the French

Royal family with whom she enjoyed a good relationship, having been employed to tutor Louis XVI's sister. Oddly, she also made positive acquaintanceships with the other side of the divide, counting both Napoleon and Robespierre as within her circle.

In 1794 her mentor and substitute father, 'uncle' Philippe, died. He left her his collection of works. The following year she married Francois Tussaud and the couple would go on to have two children. Then, in 1802 she took her son Joseph to London to exhibit her waxworks. She was invited to become part of a show held at the Lyceum Theatre, and although financially, the move was not a huge success, circumstances combined to allow her to become even better known. The Napoleonic Wars were happening at full steam, making a return to France impossible for Marie. Trapped in Britain, she travelled the country and also to Ireland, displaying her works. Her fame spread sufficiently to merit a permanent exhibition on the top floor of the Baker Street Bazaar.

Marie Tussaud lived a long life, passing aged 88 in 1850. By then, her name was made, and her legacy established, an artist whose influence continues today. She was proof that a woman of her generation could not only make it in the arts but in business as well.

In fact, women successful in business were still exceedingly rare, but less so than before. Behind the change was the emergence of the new middle classes, made on the back of the industrial revolution. Certainly, the influence of the upper classes spread out to this emerging stratum of society. But not absolutely. The entrepreneurs who sprang like flowers in a seeded meadow might not always be the prettiest in the park, but they were tough, rich and determined to spread. Business remained a man's world, but not as exclusively as before. Most probably, this was because the expectations of women of the new middle classes were less set in stone than those of women of the upper classes. One who fitted well into this mould and who made it good herself is Eleanor Coade, a woman who mixed science, creativity and business acumen to become a leading figure of her day. Her creation, Coade stone, fell out of fashion following its brief but frantic heyday, but can still be widely seen and even, given sufficiently deep pockets, produced.

Eleanor was born in the West Country in June 1733, a while before it became the setting for the 'picturesque', the environment which inspired so much art beloved of Regency gentlemen and ladies. Her father was a wool merchant, but the family moved from Exeter to London, and once there, Eleanor set up a business of her own, which sold linen.

Quite how she managed to move from this industry to that of artificial stone is sadly not recorded for posterity. Perhaps she simply spotted a business opportunity. Whatever, after her father died, the thirty-six-year-old entrepreneur purchased an artificial stone business. The original owner, Daniel Pincot, became her business partner for a couple of years while she learned the tools of the trade and helped to turn the once ailing business around. Then she sacked him while also seeking to improve upon the recipe he used. Her timing could not have been better. Her creation, Coade stone, bore many characteristics perfect for the Regency tastes, holding elaborate art and fine architecture to the fore. It was almost totally resistant to weathering and erosion and extremely versatile, working well for garden furnishings, statues, and even fine detail on buildings.

Every top architect and every leading designer wished to work in Coade stone. Several hundreds of the statues her factory produced, often neo-classical in nature, survive, and can be found across the world, from Russia to Brazil. Inevitably, Eleanor became incredibly wealthy. She never married, although in vogue with the times adopted the title Mrs, as in Mrs Coade. Such a heading was often assumed by women tackling a man's world but without a man by their side. Marriage implied respectability in the eyes of people, while being single, unless young, suggested a character fault on the part of the woman. She was a great philanthropist and advocate for poor women. She bequeathed many gifts to women in her will, stipulating that the sums were for them and not to be touched by their husbands.

Eleanor died in 1821, and without her drive and commitment, her business began to fall from fashion. Trends changed and the firm eventually folded in the 1840s. Her private life remained private, and little in the way of detail exists today. Nevertheless, to survive in a business world dominated by men and to have chosen a particularly male aspect of commercial life is evidence of the strength of character and independence of this remarkable woman.

But as astonishing as her achievements might have been, Eleanor was not the only woman of her time to succeed in what was seen and protected as a male domain. Another who achieved remarkable and surprising success is Sarah Guppy. In many ways, Sarah was a typical woman of her time and class. As with Eleanor, she was born (in 1770) into wealth created on the back of the Industrial Revolution. Her father, a rich Birmingham merchant, traded in sugar. Again, in a similar way to Eleanor, being a member of the middle rather than upper classes means that history did little to preserve details of her upbringing, despite the incredible success she was to gain. Or, maybe, the aristocratic men who wrote history chose to ensure that it focused on their gender and their class. However, we have some details of her life. Sarah married another merchant, again a wealthy man, in 1795. Once more, the conventions of the middle classes sought to follow those of the upper echelons. Samuel Guppy's business was based in Bristol, a city which was the centre of innovation and change during that period. Among their close friends in the wealthy set to which they belong is a certain Isambard Kingdom Brunel. Another is Thomas Telford, although he may have been a family friend rather than one directly of Sarah. Meanwhile, she is a dutiful wife, typical of her time. She entertains well, is good company, gets on with life quietly and produces six children. But Sarah also develops an interest in engineering.

We do not know when this fascination takes hold of her, although as a woman dependent on her husband, he must have supported her in her endeavours. But what we do know is that her biggest achievement significantly predates both Telford and Brunel – the latter is just five years old when in 1811, Sarah patents a new way of building bridges. Her approach eschewed the sort of traditional design which relied heavily on the arch. Instead, her bridges are supported by piles driven deeply into the earth. We say Sarah patented her idea. That is not strictly true. At the time, women were not permitted to patent an idea in their own name. Perhaps that is why both Brunel and Telford, who later (with her permission, to a greater or lesser degree) incorporated her ideas into their own engineering wonders, did so without reference to her. They were happy enough to take advantage of her ideas but too proud to admit the influence a woman had on their designs.

In fact, Sarah's successes were not limited to bridge building. She filed (with her husband's necessary support) no less than ten patents over the years, including one to prevent barnacles from sticking to a ship's hull. That one went down well with the Royal navy. Remarkably, one of her ideas might have been the first-ever Teasmade. She designed a machine that not only made tea but also cooked eggs and even kept plates warm. For a bit of variety, she also became a published author.

Sadly, though, Sarah's life took an unexpected turn for the worse. Her husband, who had supported her in every endeavour throughout her life, died in 1830. Sarah was a very wealthy woman by then but made a hugely unwise choice. She married Richard Eyre-Coote, a man twenty-eight years her junior. As much as Samuel Guppy is an unusually forward-thinking and enlightened man for his time, Eyre-Coote is the opposite. He works his way through his wife's money, leaving her almost broke before she decides to leave this wastrel. If ever a man married for his wife's money, it is him. She was seventy-two by then and did manage to spend her last ten years living quietly alone in Clifton, near Bristol. There, perhaps, to look on the suspension bridge which Brunel designed, employing some, if not many, of her own ideas.

That wonderful construction is a fitting legacy to a woman who first embraced the limits and expectations Regency society placed on her, then outshone them, certainly with the help and support of her husband. Firstly she worked with a good man before, so sadly, succumbing to the abuses of the worst kind of men and falling to their exploitation. Still, Sarah has the last laugh. Her patent achieved immortality in the shape of the Clifton Suspension bridge (it should be noted that there is some contention over the extent of her patent's involvement in this) and the Menai Straits bridge. Even if the names of Brunel and Telford are the ones which achieved fame through those constructions. Few of us have heard of Richard Eyre-Coote, and thank goodness for that. Plus, as Sarah modestly said herself: 'It is unpleasant to speak of oneself; it may seem boastful, particularly in a woman.'[24] At the time, she was solving the problem of how to stabilise a railway embankment.

Sarah truly was both a woman of her time and better than her time.

Another who held incredible influence is Lady Hester Stanhope. Hester was born into high privilege in 1776. Her father is Charles, Earl Stanhope, and her mother is the daughter of the former Prime Minister, William Pitt the Elder. For all this, life for this entitled woman is far from a bed of roses. Her mother dies when she is just four, and her father's behaviour is renowned for its eccentricity. A leading politician of his day, his work in the House is famed in equal parts for its excessive passion and its ineffectiveness.

At the age of twenty-four, Lady Hester went to live with her grandmother, Lady Chatham. All the better to enjoy pursuits fitting to her wit, intelligence and love for adventure. As much as a woman in her position could ever do, she eschewed the conventions of the time. A short-lived period of calm existed between England and France in 1802, following the Peace of Amiens. Lady Hester took the opportunity to travel abroad, all the better, to widen her horizons. While she was there, her grandmother died. On her return, she had no wish to live with her now unpredictable father and instead moved in with another William Pitt, this time the Younger, who until recently had also been Prime Minister. Now, as Lord Warden of the Cinque Ports, he enjoyed the grace and favour home of Walmer Castle in Kent.

This is an exciting time for a woman who yearns to be in the fast lane of life. She acts as a sort of unofficial, non-romantic wife to her uncle, becoming his social hostess. In 1804, Pitt the Younger is once again Prime Minister, and Lady Hester's involvement in political life becomes even heavier. Often, she stays with him at 10 Downing Street. She loves nothing more than meeting with powerful men. Relations with France having deteriorated once more, she can frequently be found entertaining military leaders.

Then matters take a turn for the worse. A failed romance with another politician, Granville Leveson, perhaps suggests that her toughness does not linger too far below the surface. Following the breakup, she travels for a lengthy stay at Walmer Castle and reportedly attempts suicide while there. But her strength of character sees her through this temporary crisis – she applies herself to improving the grounds of the castle and gradually returns both it and herself to their former state. Those of a fine building and a strongly spoken, determined woman.

Unfortunately, another disaster loomed on the horizon. Her uncle died, and although he had arranged for Parliament to pay her a pension, ensuring that as a single woman she could retain her independence, she lost touch with the corridors of power. This was 1806, and the following year she fell in love once more, developing a relationship with General Sir John Moore. But good fortune eludes Lady Hester. Two years later, the General is killed at the Battle of Corunna, along with her half-brother. She keeps the blood-covered glove, which is the closest memento to her lost love's death, close by her side for the rest of her life.

It is once more that indefinable strength of character which breaks Lady Hester out of her mourning. She was a woman happiest when busy, one entertained by adventure. Therefore, she decides to travel abroad once more. This time, her destination will be well beyond France. She selects a doctor, Charles Meryon, to be her companion, and together, they set sail. Over the next two years, she and the good doctor, along with another traveller she meets en route, visit Malta, Greece, Constantinople, Egypt and the Middle East, which is a part of the Ottoman Empire of the day. She even survives a Mediterranean shipwreck. The traveller, called Michael Bruce, becomes more than a companion. Soon the two are lovers.

If women were put down in Britain during this period, that was nothing compared to how women were treated in the Middle East. Despite the heat, a woman must be covered from head to toe, her face veiled. Lady Hester was not going to submit to that. Instead, she dresses as would a wealthy local man, wearing a waistcoat, pantaloon trousers and even a turban. A woman in her position is able to get away with this, with even the rulers she meets accepting her choices. Maybe they are impressed by her audacity. Whether a woman without her background could have gotten away with poking a finger in the eye of accepted cultural norms is open to question.

She embraces life in the Ottoman Empire, much as she had during her days at the Prime Minister's side. Whether making dramatic entrances on horseback, searching out buried treasure or giving gifts to local warlords, Lady Hester is a forerunner of the classic colonial Englishwoman abroad. Reports say she was adored both by ordinary people as well as leaders of the region. Maybe. Maybe not. Sources of evidence might not be that reliable. Mostly this evidence comes from Dr Meryon's own memoirs, which are hardly unbiased. It also suited the British establishment for a woman like Lady Hester, one of their own, to be seen as an eccentric but powerful personality.

Maintaining this lifestyle abroad, even when financed by her pension from Parliament, takes its toll. She falls into debt. Never one to worry about making enemies, she also manages to create a rather significant one in the form of perhaps the most powerful man of the region, Mehmet Ali, who is the Ottoman Pasha of Egypt. When Lady Hester offers sanctuary to a rival faction in the unrest, which often besieges the region, her life begins to unravel. Ali feels that her actions favour his enemies. Who knows what measures he may have instigated against the Englishwoman had her lingering contacts in the political world not stepped in? As it is, Ali forces her to repay her debts, redirecting her pension to pay off what she owes.

The adventurer is now devoid of income, and she finds that in being thus, her influence and popularity disappear. She dies, destitute, at her home on Mount Lebanon. A life wasted, or a life enjoyed? Some will think this is a tough call, but it cannot be denied that Lady Hester shows that women can have the character to stand out in a man's world. Even one as singularly male as the East of those days. She demonstrates that a woman can deny conventions. And in becoming a female of influence in a culture that allowed no such thing, Lady Hester advances the cause of women globally, well beyond the usual borders of Britain or Europe.

Most of the women we have met so far either came from the upper or middle classes, with all the advantages these implied. And, admittedly, restrictions as well. Those from the emerging middle classes had fathers who were professionals or businessmen. But what of women from the poorest of backgrounds? While the working classes made up the overwhelming majority of the population in Regency Britain – something true since those times and before them – few of their stories are recorded.

One person who bucks that trend is Mary Anning. Her home was the Dorset coast, the beautiful area around Lyme Regis, which is now, thanks to Mary, famous as the Jurassic Coast. Walk along the beaches anywhere from Exmouth in the west to Swanage in the east, and not only are the views stunning, but the cliffs are full of fossils, many of which date from the age of the dinosaur. Perhaps the most famous part of this living history is located at Charmouth, where fossil hunters can find examples literally at their feet. The beach there is littered with clearly visible fossilised remains.

The Jurassic coast is a World Heritage site these days. In fact, it is England's only such naturally occurring site. To preserve the cliffs and protect history from destruction, there are strict rules around where fossils can be collected. They must be lying loose on the beach and not dug from the cliffs. This was, of course, not the case when Mary Anning was alive.

Mary was born in 1799, entering a world of poverty. Her family were isolated, religious dissenters. They were protestants but had separated from the Church of England. So great was their poverty that of the ten (some say nine) children of Richard and Molly Anning, only two – including Mary – survived to become adults.

Richard's work was as a cabinet maker. But he was also an enthusiastic fossil collector. Little Mary loved nothing more than to wander the beaches, poking among the cliffs, at her father's side. This was her education; little or nothing in the way of formal schooling took place. Nevertheless, Mary was a bright girl who learned to read and understood both geology and anatomy. One wonders how many educated, wealthy young gentlemen travelled to her part of the South West to capture the picturesque coastline. Ostentatiously so, with the production of the latest easels and best paints. Beholding all and seeing nothing. Meanwhile, Mary went about her business. That business was collecting fossils, taking them home and cleaning them so they might be displayed in her father's shop, there to be sold to passing trade, the pennies they fetched keeping the family alive.

Mary was just ten or eleven when her world was turned upside down. Richard died suddenly, succumbing to tuberculosis. Now the already desperately poor family had no source of income. Mary's brother Joseph took an apprenticeship as an upholsterer, but the pay was meagre, and debts mounted. In the end, Mary was forced to sell her own collection of fossils in order to keep the bailiff from their door.

In a way, the Napoleonic wars, which flared just over the waters, served the Anning family well. They probably kept them alive. As we know, the South West became the favoured destination for the wealthy of London and the home counties. They would flock to the region, and Lyme Regis, with its incredible rock formations and sweeping vistas, was one of their favourite destinations. These tourists were people with money to burn. When you can afford almost anything, the unusual becomes appealing. Fashionable homes were to become decorated with the curious, and popular among these were the fossils found along the Jurassic coast. Certainly, such trinkets were so numerous that anybody with half an eye could wander the beaches and collect their own. Many did. But neatly polished examples ready for purchase also found a ready market. Mary's fossils kept the family in a home and put food on the table. Particularly popular with wealthy tourists were the 'Ammon's horns' (ammonites) and 'devil's fingers' (belemnites) which were common around Lyme Regis. Mary knew that, and she knew where to find them.

In fact, it was brother Joseph who made the discovery which would bring fame to Mary Anning. The boy discovered a large, fossilised skull that he did not recognise. Inevitably, the find piqued Mary's interest, and she spent the following months slowly, carefully digging out the fossilised remains of this creature, one that had never been seen before.

The task went on and on. The creature was incredibly large. In fact, it was over seventeen feet long. When confronted with the unknown, it is human nature to rationalise. Scientists descended on the site of Mary's excavation and came up with a simple explanation. And one that was totally incorrect. The creature, they determined, was a crocodile. Somehow, one that had travelled thousands of miles outside of its natural habitat. We can have sympathy with these finely educated men. After all, Mary was a girl and a very poor, working-class one at that. How could one such as this be expected to have made an earth-shattering discovery? It would be many years before scientists, led by Georges Cuvier, the father of palaeontology, confirmed that the beast was not a crocodile but something none had seen before.

It was named an ichthyosaur, which translates to 'fish lizard'. We now know Mary's find had lived around 200 million years before its discovery. Mary continued to make significant findings. In 1823 she came across the complete skeleton of a Plesiosaurus, the first person ever to do so. The reaction from the scientific world was sad but predictable. It must be a fake. A woman could not make such a find. Although, quite how one fakes a giant fossilised skeleton buried in sand and rock, nobody was prepared to say.

Her treatment by the educated, male scientific community was outrageous. The hypocrisy shown towards her was quite breath-taking. Mary would make the discoveries and clean them with the minutest care and attention to detail. Scientists would then travel to Lyme Regis, buy these perfectly prepared fossils off her, and claim the discoveries as their own. It was as though there was no concept that a woman, a working-class one at that, was capable of changing our perception of our past even though the evidence that she was doing so was there before the nation's eyes. There, large and extremely visible. This is not to suggest that these scientific men were deliberate plagiarists or cheats by any other name. Just at the time, it was a truth not even worth questioning that people could only make great discoveries of certain characteristics. Specifically, their gender and their social class.

The plesiosaurus is a perfect example. Even Cuvier denied that her find could be real. A special meeting of the Geological Society of London was convened. One would have thought that the most important witness at this gathering of the great and the good would be Mary herself. She was uninvited. In fact, despite being the foremost expert on dinosaurs of her day, she was never admitted to the society. No woman was; it would be another eighty years before such equality was offered to women.

At the meeting, the skeleton was identified as being genuine. Cuvier was prepared to own up to his own error of judgement but to give credit for the find to Mary? Not a chance.

Her great discoveries were not yet over. Five years after finding her plesiosaurus, she made perhaps the most remarkable, certainly strangest, the unearthing of all. The creature had a long tail and strangely constructed bone formations. In fact, she had uncovered a dimorphodon, an early flying dinosaur.

It was not just her spectacular finds that Mary contributed to science, albeit uncredited at the time. She also undertook her own study of coprolites – faeces – something which the male scientific community had up to then ignored.

Mary's finds inspired a fascination for dinosaur life which continues to this day. How many of us have wandered into the entrance hall of the Natural History Museum, perhaps as a child, and immediately found ourselves struck dumb by the sight which greets us? How many have thrilled at the Jurassic Park film franchise? For that, and for all the children and adults who over the years have spent hours collecting, studying and making anything to do with dinosaurs, we can thank Mary.

At the time, though, few were offering their gratitude. Mary was inspiring a pastime – an educational, scientific one at that. Museums displayed finds and could not cope with the public interest. Minds that were not as fine as they thought debated history. We were still many years short of Charles Darwin's seminal work, 'On the Origin of the Species', but debate raged. Mary, meanwhile, still lived in poverty.

She did have her supporters, however. Henry De la Beche was a well-known geologist and talented painter. His friend's discoveries inspired him to paint 'Duria Antiquior – A More Ancient Dorset'. This was in 1830 and was probably the first attempt to record a scene from prehistoric life. The painting was exceedingly popular, and De la Beche sold prints of his creation, using the monies raised to help support Mary, and allow her to continue her work. For all that, the greatest contributor to the world's understanding of its prehistoric natural history lived a life never out of poverty – disaster always a potential and unwanted visitor to her door. Meanwhile, others made their fame and fortune on the back of her work. She died, aged just 47 in 1847, a victim of breast cancer. She never married.

Another woman whose contribution to the world of science is noteworthy is Caroline Herschel. This German lady enjoyed an incredibly long life for her time. Born in 1750, she lived until 1848 and was the first ever professional lady astronomer. But her long life is made even more remarkable by the fact she only just made it to adulthood. She was born into a family of strong but opposing views. Her father was Isaac Herschel, a musician committed to giving his children the best chances in life. That meant education. Meanwhile, her mother, Anna, was illiterate and happy to be so. To her, a woman's place was in the home. The only education she believed a daughter needed was how to be the best wife. Caroline was born and brought up in Hanover, but at the age of three, she contracted smallpox. Survival came with the price of a pockmarked, scarred face. If that were not enough, at eleven, she fell victim to typhus. Once more, she survived, but at a great physical cost. Her growth was stunted. To a mother whose main aim for her daughters was for them to marry – ideally well - these twin consequences of illness were devastating. Caroline would never, she was sure, find the husband her mother wanted for her. So rather than try, her daughter was put into service, at her own home. She became the family's maid.

Her many siblings had, it seemed, greater ambitions for a girl who was talented, if completely uneducated. When Caroline was twenty-two her brother William decided that enough was enough. By then, he had emigrated to England and set up home in Bath, where he was a successful musician. He taught, played the church organ and even gave concerts. His proposal was that Caroline would come to live with him in the soon-to-be Regency-influenced city, where he would train her as a singer. In return, he would pay for his mother to employ an alternative servant.

The deal was done, and Caroline found herself in a new but equally challenging world. She spoke no English, had almost no education and had received no musical training. William changed that. He taught her English, maths – no breakfast was complete without a few problems to solve – and singing. She also learned to dance. The hard work from both paid off, and within five years, Caroline was becoming known as a talented soprano, even singing the lead in Handel's 'Messiah'.

As his sister's reputation grew, William's drive continued. But it shifted from music to astronomy. He set about learning the heavens and, to do so, constructed his own telescope. Then, in 1781, William spied something very large and relatively near in the skies. Yet, also, something astonishingly never previously discovered. He found Uranus. The most remarkable thing about his achievement was not so much that he had made it but that nobody had discovered it before him because Uranus is large enough to be visible to the naked eye. With that being the case, astronomers wondered what else might be out there.

King George III lobbied to give William a salary so he could give up his music and commit full time to astronomy. The King agreed, and William moved to Datchet, a small town close to Windsor from where he could be close to the monarch. There was only one problem.

William was a good brother, but times dictated that even one as enlightened as to educate his sister also assumed that a woman's job was to serve a man. To be fair to him, his mother would have instilled such beliefs from birth, and society reinforced them.

So he took Caroline with him, assuming she would be happy to give up her own musical career, thus abandoning the fame she was beginning to enjoy. She did so but very reluctantly.

'I was to be trained for an assistant astronomer,' she wrote later. 'And by way of encouragement, a telescope adapted for sweeping the night skies was given to me. I was to sweep for comets. But it was not till the last two months of the same year before I felt the least encouragement for spending the starlight nights on a grass plot covered by dew or hoar frost without a human being near enough to be within call.'[25]

It transpired, however, that Caroline's capacity for learning about the heavens was as great as her ability to conquer music. By the following year's end, she had discovered no less than four comets. She was inspired. Alone, or with her brother, she went on to find no less than eight comets and countless nebulae. So impressed was the King that he was minded to give her a pension, making her the first professional female astronomer. Over their lives, the siblings increased the number of known nebulae from around a hundred to two and a half thousand.

Their achievements are made greater by the conditions under which they worked. Not only did they build their own equipment, but the data available at the time was often wrong. To this end, Caroline spent two years correcting the mistakes in the 'British Catalogue of Stars', thus helping countless other astronomers in their studies.

She worked well into old age. Aged 75, her nephew – William's son – decided to update the existing catalogue of nebulae. An enormous undertaking. Caroline stepped out of retirement to help. She re-catalogued the data already held, listing by position rather than class of nebulae, making rediscovery much easier for her relative. That undertaking won her the British Royal Astronomical Society's Gold Medal.

Her mother was correct in one respect, Caroline never married. But her devotion to her brother was huge. When he married, Caroline was devastated, and it took time for her to come to terms with the fact that there was another woman in William's life. But, as with music first and astronomy later, Caroline adapted, and the two women became close. Without children of her own, Caroline became devoted to John Herschel, the nephew for whom she later came out of retirement. When her brother died, leaving her a substantial income in his will, she decided to return to Hanover. There she lived, a sprightly old woman, until her peaceful death on January 9th, 1848, aged 97. She was buried in the local church, next to the graves of her parents. With her in her coffin, she took a lock of William's hair.

The Regency is a remarkable period of history. One iniquity, however, stood out perhaps more than any other. Britain's involvement in the slave trade. In the next chapter, we will look in much closer detail at this injustice. But we can finish this chapter by looking at a woman who did much to alleviate the dreadful conditions in which slaves existed and who brought to wider attention the evil of this practice.

Our final participant in our chapter on women who made a difference is one who used her position and influence to support many of the most vulnerable in Regency society. That is Annabella Milbanke, the future Lady Byron. Annabella was born in 1792 and emerged into life full of privilege. But also an awareness of social justice. Her father was Sir Ralph Milbanke, a Whig MP who advocated for the abolition of slavery. Along with his wife, Judith, Sir Ralph ensured that his daughter grew up to understand the importance of support for the poor and an end to slavery. Annabella was an intelligent girl with interests in mathematics and astronomy. She studied the latter with a Cambridge tutor.

She met her future husband in 1812. Always a controversial figure, Lord Byron was by then active in the House of Lords, where he opposed the Frame Breaking Bill, a controversial move which would have seen the death penalty cast on many Luddites. He was also a strong advocate of social reform. On the other hand, famously, Lord Byron was inordinately attracted to women, even his own half-sister. His rampant obsession with having affairs was considered so extreme, even by Regency standards, that he became ostracised from society. (We will look at Byron's affairs in more detail in a later chapter.)

So when the poet proposed marriage to Annabella, she sensibly refused. Lord Byron, though, was a hard man to turn down, and when his second proposal arrived in 1814, she agreed. The marriage was a mistake. Together they had a daughter, but Byron continued his sexual infidelities, with Annabella declaring him to be insane. In turn, he referred to his wife as a 'moral Clytemnestra'. The joys of having an intellectual husband. Their marriage lasted under two years, with Annabella escaping his wandering clutches and taking their daughter with her.

If Annabella was damaged by the experience, and it is hard to see how she wouldn't be, it did not distract her from her good work. Education and social support were two of the mantras by which she lived her life. She set up a school in Ealing, gave over the ground floor of her Brighton house for the education of mechanics, and helped set up a branch of the Cooperative Society to aid those on low incomes.

She was also an ardent anti-slavery campaigner. But with a painful irony that seemed to elude those in charge at the time, this movement which sort to free others from chains and give them a voice, did not allow women to speak. Only men. In fact, even a painting celebrating the anti-slavery movement failed to include women among its subjects, despite the movement being reliant on female support.

Perhaps, though, her most successful campaigns lay in improving the conditions in the slums and increasing rights for women. She worked closely with the social reformer Mary Carpenter who had begun reformatories for girls. She fought for orphans, arguing that it was society's duty to care for such unfortunates rather than see them cast out to live, or more often die, on the streets. She fought for education for the poor. She founded a vocational school in Ockham, Surrey.

Lady Byron died in May 1860, having spent almost all her life working for the poor. Her parents would have been proud of her. Annabella Byron demonstrates, perhaps more than anybody else of her time, that while a woman might not be able to determine the life into which she is born, she can use those advantages she is given for good. Just as William Lavery, the Quaker preacher, advocated, albeit to a different audience. Such actions and commitments help to make the lives of others so much better than they might otherwise have been. They do so in more ways than one. On an individual level, through specific assistance, but also on a wider scale through campaigns for social justice.

Despite the conventions of Regency Britain, Lady Byron's life, and those of many others in this chapter, demonstrate that society does not have to be a closed shop, to replicate itself to the benefit of the rich and titled and to the detriment of the poor. Such a social and political position has always been controversial. Some might argue that it is particularly so today. Nevertheless, when one is born with advantages in life, such as a talent, a strong personality or wealth, it can be used to help others, and not just oneself.

There is a footnote to Lady Byron's life, which leads us into the next chapter. In 1850, with slavery now abolished, Ellen and William Craft arrived in Britain. They were escaped slaves and were encouraged to speak at a number of meetings about their experiences. The two were given a chance to start their lives anew in Britain, and thanks to Lady Byron and places given to them at her Ockham school, they were able to learn to read and write and start a business of their own - a lodging house – in London.

CHAPTER 7

CASTING OFF THE CHAINS: BLACK WOMEN OF THE REGENCY

King George III's wife looked, to all intents and purposes, like a white woman. It is highly unlikely that he would have been allowed to marry her if she did not. Even among the list of strong characters who have been Queen of England, she stands out as a tough old bird. Charlotte ruled her palace with an iron will. She was strict and demanding but also deeply in love with her errant husband. Yet it seems that her past contained a hereditary line which makes its way from North Africa. During a time when slavery is the camel upon which Britain secures its wealth, its queen is a black woman.

We need to head back to the thirteenth century to find the most likely explanation for Queen Charlotte's mixed-race ancestry. There we find ourselves in Portugal, under the rule of Alfonso III. By all accounts, he is a pretty good King, demonstrating sensitivity towards the uncertain political climate of the time and paying good heed to the concerns of the middle classes. That, in turn, leads him to make a number of decisions which generally, history records, make life better for his people.

Alfonso married twice and had a number of affairs. It is his relationship with Madragana, or Mor Afonso, which concerns us most. Because Madragana is most probably of African descent, it is likely, but not certain, that she is a North African, a Moor, and together with Alfonso III, she has two children.

We need to move on fifteen generations to reach Queen Charlotte, and by then, her African genes have been heavily diluted. Nevertheless, her marriage to George does provide a (fairly) conclusive link back to African heritage.

However, what we can say with absolute certainty is that Queen Charlotte's life was vastly different to that experienced by other black women in Britain at the time. Yet the story of black people in Regency Britain is not as simple as it might appear. Not all are slaves, and even the legality of slavery is hard to determine. Nobody is sure of the actual number of black people in Britain under the rule of George III and into the Regency period. Most have arrived somewhere down their generations as a result of the slave trade and probably number somewhere between 10000 and 20000. To give perspective, a census held in 1801 showed that just over 10 million people in total lived in England and Wales at that time. We know that the ratio between men and women for black people was in the region of two to one, so it seems a fair conclusion to estimate that around 5000 black women were living in the UK when the census was taken.

Whilst most of these women live in absolute poverty, and many continue in their slavery to a lesser or greater degree, that is not the case for all. Many black women worked in service, but others did own property, and some were traders. More still lived as wives to white men. In fact, slavery in Britain was regarded as something like the waste product of a manufacturing process. It was a necessary evil to further the empire, and many made their fortunes on the back of it. Yet, at the same time, it was a subject on which few really wished to be drawn. For all that, the abolitionist movement remained strong. The law allowed for slavery without ever really establishing the abhorrent act in statute. This led to confusion, and out of this uncertainty, some black women did carve for themselves a reasonable life. But for every Dido Elizabeth Belle, who became an heiress and was taken in by a man of property and means, there were plenty who shared the trials of the likes of Ann Duck, a black woman forced into prostitution and criminality, and who was executed in 1744.

When we trawl through historical information, we find that very little on record about the lives of black women of the Regency period. Those who can be traced are usually ones who created some kind of scandal, such as Ann Duck above. The reason for this absence of data seems clear. Racism abounded in British society at the time. The only way a black woman might live even a mildly reasonable life was to abandon her own cultural heritage and assimilate herself into British society. In other words, to become metaphorically white and thus disappear amongst her Caucasian contemporaries. Evidence of this attempted assimilation is found in the records of baptisms. Black women were overwhelmingly given popular English names of the day. Names such as Ann, Mary or Elizabeth.

For the poorest, the effective slavery they endured meant that their only possible hope of some form of freedom involved running away from white society, whereas the small number of black women who actually achieved some degree of wealth sought to adopt the prevailing trends of femininity in order to become accepted within their circles. Although not every black woman abandoned her roots. Catherine Despard, for example, was the wife of a politically radical army officer, Colonel Despard, yet seems to have done everything behaviourally possible to retain her roots and become, in effect, a black woman in white society.

Yet even against this backdrop of cultural negation and discrimination, some women still emerge in their own right. Indeed, a character such as Dido Elizabeth Belle does offer us a picture of how a black woman might experience a different sort of life. She was born in 1761 as the illegitimate daughter of a slave, Maria Bell, and a senior officer in the Royal Navy, Sir John Lindsay. Lindsay, it seems, took his responsibilities seriously, or at least members of his wider family did. His uncle was William Murray, the 1st Earl of Mansfield, who also happened to be the Lord Chief Justice. As we have mentioned before, legality over the slave trade was complex in Britain, and one of Murray's tasks was determining that legality in the many cases brought before his courts.

The earl took Dido in, and she was able to live in the magnificent Kenwood House, which sits on the edge of Hampstead Heath. What was perhaps even more remarkable was that Murray took in this great niece, along with another, Elizabeth Murray, as a member of the family rather than seeking to use her as a servant. That such an open-minded, and forward-thinking man should also be Lord Chief Justice augers well for freedoms at the time.

We do not know how Sir John Lindsay and Maria Bell met. (She gained the 'e' we see at the end of her daughter's surname later.) Most probably, it was in the Caribbean, in which case this would be where Maria lived as a slave. Other sources suggest Sir John may have captured a Spanish ship on which she worked, again under the ownership of another. If this is vague, at least more information exists around her age when the two met. She was around 15 at this time. It seems that Lindsay remained in contact with Maria, supporting her and the child. Certainly, by the stage that Dido was five, she and her mother were living in England. We know that because her baptism is recorded in St George's, a church in Bloomsbury. Interestingly, Lindsay chose not to be recorded as the father. However, when Dido is around the age of thirteen, records show that her mother is a free woman and has been given a plot of land in America to build a new life.

Sir John, meanwhile, sired at least three or four more illegitimate children with mothers of African heritage. If he actually fathered this number, then the implication is that he had relationships with many more. Not every encounter was likely to produce a baby. Perhaps he kept these other children secret from his family, or perhaps they thought they had done enough in taking in Dido. Whatever, these other children seemed to have remained in Jamaica.

Dido, meanwhile, was offered the same opportunities as Murray's other great niece. She was educated and prepared for life among the social elite of the upper classes. She was even granted an allowance. When John Lindsay died, the London Chronicle noted of his illegitimate daughter that her 'amiable disposition and accomplishments have gained her the highest respect from all his Lordship's relations and visitants.'[26]

Such a compliment raises an interesting question. Was Regency racism and discrimination more about class prejudice than the colour of a person's skin? Certainly, in Lord Mansfield's case, black people had a powerful advocate. Maybe this was, in part, a result of his close relationship with Dido. There was clearly great affection between the pair, and the beautiful young woman cared for him in his dotage. However, while the Lord Chief Justice is recorded as describing the slave trade as 'odious', even he had his hands tied to an extent. Britain's wealth and global power were inextricably tied to this shocking practice. Nevertheless, he did what he could. Perhaps his most important act was to rule that slave traders could not force any slave to leave the country in order to be sent to work elsewhere. A point that seems particularly apt as the current British Government seeks to send black refugees out of the country should they seek asylum here.

He also clearly feared for what his niece's future might be after his death, making it clear in his will that Dido was a free woman. That document also made sure she was looked after financially. Perhaps not as much as his other great-niece, but still generously. Of course, we do not know for sure the reason behind him granting Dido a lesser sum. It could have been racially motivated, but it was more likely just that the trend of the times was to grant illegitimate relations a smaller inheritance than those born within wedlock. Something that applied whatever the colour of their skin.

Dido was given an annual allowance of £100 and a lump sum of £500, which is the equivalent of around £40000 today. Enough on which to live comfortably for sure. However, and history does not record a reason for this, she did move down the social ladder after her great uncle's death. Hopefully, only because she fell in love. She married a steward called John Davinier, and the two lived quietly and comfortably, producing three sons until Dido died at the early age of 43. Perhaps she never regained the grandeur of the Kenwood years but compared to the overwhelming majority of black women in England at that time, she lived a good life.

Dido's life bears some similarities with that of Catherine Despard, although this woman of Jamaican descent was much more public in her drive for social change. We see in Dido's life the intention to assimilate into British upper-class society that we have already mentioned, and how this then probably proves impossible once her mentor and great uncle dies. Of course, it may be that Dido chose her route towards a quieter existence, but if so, this is something Catherine certainly eschews. She is, with her husband, a committed abolitionist. And that makes her a danger to people who wield power.

Colonel Despard is everything the British elite fear most. As an abolitionist, he threatens their wealth; as an Irishman, he is confusingly both a natural enemy and an ally; as a high-ranking military officer, he is also one of them. If that is not enough to cause inbred minds to boil, he is also married to a black woman. Proudly and openly so. This is not some marriage of convenience but a marriage of love, respect and mutual affection.

It is of little surprise that not much history exists to explain how a white male British officer came to marry a black woman in the late 1700s. But we can make educated guesses. During the middle part of the 1780s, Colonel Despard was charged with finding a site for a new British settlement somewhere in the Caribbean or in central America. This involves his ship circling the waters of Jamaica. Tropical illnesses abound, and it seems a more than fair bet that at some time, the good Colonel should succumb to some unpleasant disease or other. One to which his body offers little natural immunity. Perhaps Catherine nurses him back to health. Or perhaps he meets her while he is recuperating on the island. We do not know how old she is at this time since we have no idea when she was born.

Some reports suggest she may be the daughter of a preacher. Maybe he is so close to death as to need some spiritual help. It seems as though her mother is definitely Jamaican and is a free black woman on the island, living close to the capital.

Despard really is a remarkable man for his time, and his story is a complex one. He is a fine sailor and a great military leader who is awarded the Governorship of an area of what is now Belize, which back then was identified as the Mosquito Coast. It is an odd and inhospitable place, one which the Spanish have ceded to England. It is largely English anyway. The harsh terrain is populated by former soldiers and sailors, tough men who barely scrape an existence from the land. The Government orders that Despard bring them together into this new region and offer them parcels of land as an incentive to up sticks and move.

Among this collection of the poor, the cut-throat, and former slaves are a group men known as the Baymen. Unlike their contemporaries, these are rich men whose fortune is made from the mahogany trade. When Despard awards them no greater share of the land than the natives and the slaves who live nearby, outrage ensues.

These powerful interests go straight to the British Government, demanding that the interests of black and Latin people be regarded as less important than their own. Despard responds that he must act by the law of England since the new territory is now considered to be English. English law, he states, allows no such formal division of awards along the lines of race. He is correct, although more by his exact interpretation of the written word than by its application. The Baymen continue to protest, arguing that their industry will be destroyed. When a new Home Secretary takes charge, matters accelerate towards a head. William Wyndham Grenville suspends Despard. The former military man responds by standing as a magistrate in the new colony. He is voted in on a landslide. The Baymen argue that this is only because he gives a vote to black and poor people. Democracy in Georgian times is fine, it seems, provided it delivers the result the rich desire.

Parliament favours the traders over justice, and Despard is ordered to return to England, there to explain himself. It turns nasty, and refusing to be bullied into racist and discriminatory action, he is arrested and accused of terrorism.

But this is a chapter about women of colour, not of white men attempting to improve justice. So what of Catherine? The answer, strangely, is that nobody knows. The Baymen have been happy to slur Despard's name by implying he is attracted to black people, but they do not mention that he has a black wife. Even his friend, his deputy and colleague, writes glowingly about Despard's qualities but does not mention Catherine.

It seems that to be married to a black woman is an act so outrageous that the blatant sensibilities of the era just do not know how to react to it. Even official records of the time, which include black people in a multitude of roles, do not include any mention of interracial marriage.

Yet, like the rampant love affairs into which men and women gladly threw themselves with abandon, interracial relationships were far from unknown, and in the colonies (as we saw with Maria Bell), white men frequently had affairs with black women, often resulting in mixed-race children. A former slave, Olaudah Equiano, was touring Britain around this time, telling his life story and advocating free and open marriage between races. Marriage being, he argued, a matter of love, not colour.

Maybe it might be considered surprising, but Equiano had found favour among some aspects of the higher echelons of British society, including the Wesleyan churches and many literary societies. Each was, in its way, highly influential. A current leading thinker on the subject, Mike Jay, certainly believes it was the influence of these two which deterred the Baymen from drawing attention to the marriage. It might, they fear, be seen as a forward-thinking action on the part of Despard rather than an outrage.[27]

Of course, by Victorian times, as the Empire (under the guise of the East India Company) committed mayhem around the world, the racial superiority of the white man was considered supreme. Even one as derided as the Colonel was about to become could not be thought to have loved a black woman. As a result, Catherine is recorded as being his housekeeper. Worse, those who do not accept this regard her as being no more than deluded in thinking the Colonel is her husband.

What follows is a human rights violation of the highest order. Determined to support the interests of wealthy traders, the Government displays no interest in justice. For more than half a decade, the Despards are victimised, pursued and sued. The Colonel ends up in a debtors' prison, and no record shows how Catherine coped – financially or emotionally - during this time. Nevertheless, the two remain true to each other. Despard is released, now an even more militant man. He becomes an ardent agitator for the abolition of the slave trade. But he is Irish, and that is the excuse the British authorities need to arrest him. Further, they accuse him of committing carnal acts with a black woman. Who is, of course, his wife. Then the Great Rebellion occurs in Ireland, and the British Government, that upholder of justice and democracy, suspends the rule of Habeas Corpus and Despard, along with other Irishmen, is held without recourse to a trial.

As we can imagine, this is a far cry from the polite dances, the conventions of romance and those romanticised paintings of the countryside through which the common perception of the Regency is portrayed.

It is while her husband is being held without trial that Catherine really comes into her own. This is a black woman fighting against an English society run by upper-class white men. The imprisoned group of Irishmen are housed in the harsh Coldbath Fields prison. Catherine lobbies Parliament for their release and even enlists the help of Sir Frances Burdett, an independent MP, to support her.

But the male hegemony is dominant. Vague threats are made against Catherine, who is accused of being turned into a mouthpiece by political opponents of the Government. Eventually, habeas corpus is restored, and Despard is released. The powers that be want it to appear as though nothing has happened. Then he is arrested once more, accused of high treason through being behind a plot to assassinate the king. It is nonsense, and he is convicted purely on the basis of evidence from informers who are in the pay of the Government. His sentence is death, and he will be hung, drawn and quartered. Publicly. The age of enlightenment? Not really.

In fact, the sentence proves how out of touch the decision-makers are with all tiers of society. When there is an outcry about the savagery of Despard's proposed punishment, they are forced to commute the sentence to one merely of hanging and beheading. Catherine continues to campaign for her husband's release, urging Lord Nelson – an advocate of his fellow sailor – to fight his corner with the king. But it is to no avail. Catherine and Despard spend their last days together, he in prison, she visiting. They continue to plan their fight. But it is a hopeless cause, and Despard is executed.

Still, Catherine fights on. She wins her husband's right to be buried in St Paul's Cathedral, this against huge opposition from the Lord Mayor of London and others. She is given a pension by Sir Frances Burdett. But white history blankets out black achievements, and little more is recorded of Catherine or her family. This line of the Despards seems to end with her son, and Catherine dies in Somers Town around 1815. Just a heroic woman who happened to be black. A campaigning black advocate of her husband and an abolitionist who happened to be a woman. She deserves more fame, as does Mary Prince (circa 1788 to 1833, or probably later).

As the first black woman ever to publish her autobiography – in English at least – she gave the world its first-hand documented source of what life could be like for a slave.

She tells of being sold. The description is almost unbearable. Her mother stands, watching on, crying, not even able to speak, as her daughters are sold like animals to the highest bidder. She has no say, no rights, no power of argument. Physical intervention is hopeless. Meanwhile, Mary is the eldest in the family and the first to be auctioned. She is handled roughly, and any remaining dignity is lost as she is humiliated by men who are thoughtless towards her own sensitivities but also no doubt aroused by their own. They can literally do what they like to this girl, provided they do not reduce her value by harming her in a lasting manner.

She is sold for fifty-seven pounds, and the gathered white crowd nod that this is a good price, like a slab of meat that has gone for more than expected. Mary was brought up in Bermuda, and was sold a number

147

of times, so by the point she reaches around the age of sixteen, she is working in Antigua as a domestic house slave. It is a sign of the poor conditions in which she lives and the severity of the work she is forced to undertake that, in the supposed prime of life, she is already suffering from rheumatism. She also marries, but when her owners, the Wood family, decide to travel to England, Mary asks to go with them, and they agree.

The law, or non-law, to be more precise, in England at the time was complicated in the extreme. It is 1828, the Abolition of the Slave Trade Act has been enshrined on vellum for more than twenty years. But contrary to beliefs held by many, slavery remains permissible in the country. Full abolition is still five years away. Although slaves cannot be bought or sold in either England or the colonies, and it is illegal to take them out of the country, it is sort of permitted to retain ownership of slaves already in servitude. The case for Mary to claim her freedom would be complicated; because although she has been with the Wood family for more than ten years, her time with them does not predate the act.

However, it is an academic point. Even if Mary leaves the Wood household, where can she go? How can she live? Nevertheless, now Mary has a say in her life, Adam Wood and his family cannot cope with a slave who refuses to be a slave. In the end, she is given a letter which states she is free to leave the household but also advises that nobody employ her. Significantly, the letter falls short of granting her freedom. Mary is made of strong stuff, and she decides to set out on her own. She takes shelter in the Moravian Church and then begins to undertake occasional work with Thomas Pringle, a writer and abolitionist. Her determination and willingness to work hard enable her to find employment on a full-time basis, and meanwhile, Thomas Pringle tries to persuade Adam Wood to manumit – formally free – Mary, but he refuses. This is significant because it means that she cannot return to Antigua and her husband without once more becoming Wood's slave. Anti-slavery sentiments are growing strongly among those in power, but too many retain interests to actually allow anything to pass which might benefit slaves themselves. Then what else do we expect? The monarch is Head of State but wields little actual political power even though his influence might mean a statement on slavery would carry some weight. It is still the Regency period; although the Regent is now King, parliament has little interest in a monarch's views – whatever they might be – and the monarch has no interest in expressing them. Despite his unpopularity, he still sets the social lead and that lead is to offer no lead - it is better to pretend to adopt the moral high ground while doing nothing than actually seek to bring about change. Not all feel that way. The abolitionists are growing in influence. But they are not there yet.

If black society is to achieve anything, it will have to do so itself. Something Mary takes on board and acts upon, unlike her supposed betters in Parliament. She petitions Parliament, the first woman of any colour to do so on the subject of anti-slavery. She writes and publishes her autobiography. It is enough, and Mary wins her freedom. Able to return to the West Indies, where she lives until her death.

We do not know much about Mary's later life, but she is a national hero in her homeland of Bermuda. The same might be said for Dorothy Kirwan Thomas and her small Caribbean home island of

Montserrat. Dorothy was born in 1756, or thereabouts, like most of her peers, into a life of slavery. Something she commits to leaving behind as soon as she is old enough to question the conditions under which she lives.

Dorothy's life could make a six-season Netflix costume drama on its own. Indeed, it is the inspiration for Vanessa Riley's novel, 'Island Queen'. Dorothy is believed to have been illiterate – something she never allowed to hold her back – so everything about her life comes from third-hand reports. Nevertheless, it is a tale of slavery, freedom, romance and success. It is a story of cut-throat politics and hypocrisy. It even includes an affair with a future King of England.

Dorothy was born to a black mother and white father, an Irish planter called John Kirwan. Despite her mixed heritage, she was clearly and strongly a black child.

Dorothy started earning money young. Dolly, or Dol as she was known in her own community, sold trinkets and small goods, making enough of an income to eventually buy her freedom. Her ambition does not stop there, and over the following years, her sisters, her mother and her own children are bought out of slavery, as she is driven by her incessant desire for freedom. The process takes her sixteen years, but Dorothy is determined, and with a goal in sight, she will reach it, no matter how long it takes.

Her ambition knows no bounds. Dorothy sets up further businesses – a housekeeping service, retail stores and even some hotels. One of these boasts a French restaurant. Dorothy expands her interests over the entire Caribbean and onto the South American mainland of Demerara – she becomes known as the Queen of Demerara for her business interests in this part of British Guiana.

The income she makes is used to ensure her own children will never suffer the ignominy she has endured. She pays for them to be educated in the United Kingdom, the girls in London and the boys in Scotland. In time her grandchildren will follow the same paths. Her life casts questions about attitudes to black people. Dressed to the nines, sporting bright clothes which symbolise her freedom, she mixes in the highest circles of the Caribbean. She must stand out so dramatically. Is she an amusement to the monied classes? Rather like Duleep Singh, the last Maharaja of Punjab would later become in Victorian England. Somebody to be feted in company and laughed at behind her back, with her outrageous clothes and her even more outrageous wealth? Or is she respected as an entrepreneur, held in high regard for having made it from the humblest, most disadvantaged of beginnings in a culture where she is not only the wrong gender but the wrong race as well?

We cannot know for sure. What does seem certain, however, is that the perceptions of others mattered little to this supremely rich self-made woman. It is at a dance in Roseau, Dominica, that the beautiful, resplendent Dorothy meets a Prince who is even more of a peacock than she. The Duke of Clarence – a man we already know as being fond of an affair, is apparently entranced by this woman. He is caricatured by James Gillray, enwrapped with a black woman in a hammock on his ship, HMS Pegasus. Satirising the rich and the royal is certainly a common enough pastime in the Regency period, as we well know. Nevertheless, usually, there will be some truth behind the savage illustrations.

Yet there may have been a darker side to this woman, one which may explain her acceptance in the elite circles of the Caribbean. It is probable that some of her fortune was built on the back of slaves she owned herself. If true, this demonstrates that Dorothy may be a great figure, but she is not a saint. Again, we enter the realm of cultural assimilation. The wealthy own slaves. Dorothy is wealthy, so she must own slaves. Perhaps at that time, in those circumstances, there was no other way for a woman to make her fortune. In all likelihood, the only way for a black woman to stay free and safe during that changeable, unpredictable period is to mix with white company and so gain the protection of white peers. Not that this is a defence against any form of slavery. Anything but. The story of her own slave-keeping is probably true. When the indefensible practice was finally abolished in Britain and the colonies, some compensation was paid to slave owners. Records show that in 1835 Dorothy received a little over £3000 (close to half a million pounds today) for the release of 67 slaves.

Dorothy travelled to England frequently, often to see her children and grandchildren. She died, in her 90th year, at her home in Demerara.

Kitty Kirkpatrick's story follows a very different line from that of Mary Prince and even Dorothy Thomas. It demonstrates that not every woman of colour endured intense hardship, although Kitty's early life is marked by unrest and tragedy. To understand her story, we must head back a generation. Her mother is a noblewoman living in Hyderabad, a Muslim facing subjugation by the marauding tentacles of the East India Company. This organisation, in many ways the British Government in disguise, is infiltrating and exploiting India, and in 1795 yet another well-placed British soldier decides to get in on the act. Colonel James Achilles Kirkpatrick will become the Resident, a sort of official ambassador, at the Indian Court of Hyderabad, and he is clear that his duty is to promote his employer's interests. Promote them at whatever cost to the native population.

Then, at the court, he meets Khair un-Nissa. He falls in love, marries her in a Muslim rather than Christian ceremony, and adopts local clothes and the culture of his new wife's home. He converts to Islam. It seems as though Khair is little more than a child, a young teen at most. As can easily be imagined, for the racists and expansionists of the East India Company, such a move is incomprehensible. Not because of Khair's age but because of her ethnicity. Their horror is compounded that this betrayal is from one of their own. This sort of assimilation of British men and, far more rarely, women into Asian culture is not unknown but is unheard of for a person in as important a position as Kirkpatrick. As a final kick into the midriff of his exploitative employers, he becomes a spy, a double agent working for the Hyderabad court.[28]

In 1802 Kirkpatrick and Khair have a daughter, Sahib Begum. Together with her elder brother, William, she enjoys the fine life of an Indian Court, happy to live as a Shia Muslim with a formerly Christian father. It is a loving, doting home but also a dangerous one. James' actions have made him vulnerable within the company, an organisation not renowned for tolerance or an open mind. Equally, mortality rates in India are high among young children, and so in

1805, the decision is made to send the youngsters to England. There they will live with William's father, confusingly also called Colonel James Fitzpatrick. Who can imagine what impact a journey across half of the world, away from their parents and into a climate and culture totally new, could have had on the three and five-year-olds? They will never see their homeland or, it transpires, their parents again. The children are baptised soon after their arrival in England, and Sahib becomes Katherine or Kitty. Then their father dies in India, and soon their mother is abandoned in disgrace by her own family, having embarked on an affair with another British colonial living in the sub-continent.

Both, though, have already bestowed great sums on their children, and they will grow up in considerable comfort. Kitty was around twenty when she met Thomas Carlyle, the philosopher and historian. He was the tutor to the children of a cousin of Kitty's, with whom she was staying at the time. Carlyle is immediately besotted. Still, ironically considering the fame he is later to achieve, Carlyle is just a poor young man at the time and not at all suited to become the husband of a rich young and mystical noblewoman. At least, that is the opinion of her British family. For Carlyle, though, the memory of his half-Indian Princess stays with him throughout his life, and she crops up both in his memoirs and in his novel, 'Sartor Resartus'.

Kitty, though, does find happiness. She marries James Winslowe Phillips, and together they enjoy thirty years of contentment, along with seven children. And, as middle age beckons, Kitty embarks on a reunion of sorts with the Indian side of her heritage, entering into correspondence with her maternal grandmother with whom she shares distant but fond memories.

Kitty lived out her final years at her villa in Torquay, maybe the sub-tropical microclimate triggering some long distant memories of her homeland. She died there in 1889.

Of course, these stories are the rarest of exceptions for black women of the Regency. What they tell us is both uplifting and sad. Enormous talent, determination and commitment were required for slaves to become free, but that was only the first step in their lives of freedom. Slavery was the elephant in the room for Regency Britain. Albeit one of many, it is true. Few approved of it, most opposed it, but the lowest number of all did anything about it. So even if a slave became free, their movement was simply from one form of intense poverty to another. Women had it tough enough anyway, black women even more so.

And that meant, for some, the only option is to become part of the society they have joined, in turn neglecting the one they have foregone. We cannot blame black women for doing this. Almost never did they have an alternative. Beyond, that is, remaining in captivity.

At the same time, society creates its own mysticism around black culture. The power balance is not all one way, even if it is mostly so. Perhaps it is fear of the different that enables this element to emerge, or perhaps a kind of reverse assimilation, the notion that there is something special about these unusual people with their strange cultures. A good story to illustrate this mysticism is the uncertain tale of Miss William Brown. Miss Brown is a sailor, a very successful one aboard the HMS Charlotte. She is small, around five feet four, but astonishingly strong and for ten years carries off the illusion that she is a man. It takes that long to come to light that William Brown is, in fact, a black woman.

As exciting as this story is, it is not borne out by evidence. It is pretty hard to believe that a woman could carry off such a deception for ten years among the close living conditions aboard a military ship of the time. And records of the HMS Charlotte demonstrate that the only William Brown aboard is a recently recruited Scotsman who is definitely not black. However, some time before, a black woman from the Caribbean was identified as trying to get employment on the ship, dressed as a man. She was quickly spotted. It is possible to see how two such unimportant facts might become stretched into an unlikely story of a black woman dressed as a man fooling the authorities for a decade and making a fine career for herself in the process.

But it takes a willingness of belief for such a story to gain credence. That willingness betrays an attitude towards ethnicity, which is not usually considered when it comes to race relations of the period.

Thus, the Regency surprises us once again.

CHAPTER 8

LESBIANS, CROSS DRESSERS AND OTHER TABOOS

We can see that there were plenty of groups who faced the worst kind of prejudice and discrimination in Regency times. While the upper classes were glorifying in their fancy clothes and elegant homes, the working class, women (in many ways, of every social stratum) and black people all faced the biggest uphill struggles to survive.

Another group of people can be added to that list of the disadvantaged. That is the LBGTQ community. Which was, it turns out, more substantial than history likes to tell. But then, that should not be a surprise. Why should the times in which we live be a factor in our sexuality? The answer is simple. They are not. However, different eras certainly influenced the lives of LBGTQ people because attitudes changed frequently over time. To be gay during the Regency was not to live in the worst of times, not by any means. But it was also not to live in a free and liberal society. Libertine, yes, but only so far. Fittingly for the Regency, even that broad conclusion has to be consumed with a good dose of dubious salt.

That is because attitudes differed enormously towards men compared to how they were held toward lesbian women. For once, women received the better end of the deal.

Certainly, homosexuality was frowned upon during Regency Britain. But with a nice blend of intolerance and hypocrisy, gay people could attend one of the many 'Molly' houses which flourished at this time. These inns and coffee shops acted as fronts for homosexual encounters. In fact, they were often situated near pillories, although whether these were placed to act as warnings or welcoming signposts is unclear. Guests would enter with the uncomfortable thought that while a visit from the authorities was unlikely, if it did take place, the consequences could be severe. In fact, it seemed as though actually being present during a raid was not a prerequisite for prosecution. Take the unfortunate John Hepburn as an example. He and his possible lover, a drummer boy thirty years his junior called Thomas White, were hung, having been convicted of sodomy. That they were almost certainly not present at neither the alleged site nor and time of their supposed liaison says as much about Regency justice as it does about the prevailing attitudes of the period.

But if men ran the risk of suffering anything between disapproving tolerance and execution for their sexuality, lesbians could pursue their romantic interests with a much greater degree of safety. Although, as we shall see, they may well still incur the ire of their neighbours. However, prosecution rarely followed the revelation that a friendship went further than genteel society. Even when the law did bear down on ladies' intimate fraternisations, it was likely to do so in a surprisingly restrained manner.

There were a number of possible reasons for this. Firstly, whilst the term 'lesbian' meant much the same in Regency parlance as it does today, there was a wide and ignorant assumption among many that such practices did not take place. Secondly, the opportunity to meet up with same-sex counterparts was limited for women. Surviving those times without a husband was a challenge for all but the richer members of society. That meant that many lesbians were married, limiting their opportunity to establish secret affairs.

Those that did decide to partner up tended to opt for one of two approaches. The more ingenious women embarked on relationships where one partner lived as a man, dressing and working as such. Then again, such an approach was risky in the extreme. Cross-dressing was seriously frowned upon, and those caught in the act would, in all likelihood, face a far more serious punishment than for anything they might receive as a result of their lesbian liaisons. As a concept, cross-dressing has been little explored in Regency Britain, but we do know that the motivation for such actions was not always sexual. Gender expectations were strong and deeply set, and for many women, the best route to further their own ambitions lay in pretending they were men. Talent and commitment were frequently not enough for anybody to make it in their chosen sphere on their own. Opportunity is also a must-have. For women, this was frequently in short supply during that era. As indeed, has been the case for much of civilised history, many would argue.

Still, there was another group of ladies who lived more openly as a couple. Such women were often monied – they had to be to support themselves. Whether it was easier for society to accept them as such or just that people did not believe women of a higher class could be lesbians, relationships in these circumstances were often considered to be no more than close friendships. That is not to simplify attitudes. The prevailing outlook towards same-sex relationships was as complex as so many other aspects of Regency society. It is a time of change and more liberal attitudes. Same-sex relationships, especially between women, are generally acceptable. Provided they are discreet, not discussed, private, unspoken, never confirmed and absolutely hidden away. The attitude is hypocritical, but at least it is more tolerant than what both predated and immediately followed it.

It is also telling how few stories of lesbian women emerge from the era. As we will see, when they do, the stories are often clouded in a mist of misplaced respectability. Genuine love becomes friendship; sex is familiarity. When women live together, they are companions. Of course, the above is bound to be true in some cases – to be a woman alone is a tricky way to live – but it is an interpretation which serves to hide love, not celebrate it.

'The people generally remark, as I pass along, how much I am like a man.'[29] The words Anne Lister records in her diary are not those of a cowed and downtrodden woman, embarrassed by her life choice. After all, it would be easier to don a pelisse and bonnet rather than endure the mockery her honesty provokes.

Because while it was true that to be a lesbian was unlikely to bring down the full weight of the law, to be openly so was to induce cruel comments. The story of Anne Lister is, therefore, extremely pertinent. In many ways, it is sad, but also, this woman's willingness to raise a metaphorical middle finger to those who criticised her is extremely inspiring. For her peers, secretly, in the quietest way possible, it must also have been liberating.

According to her diaries – she religiously kept a journal – men would send abusive letters – one went as far as to place an advertisement in the Leeds Mercury, supposedly from Anne, saying that she sought a husband. In a time when to receive a proposal of marriage meant a long pre-courtship ritual, men would shout mocking requests for her hand as she walked down the street. She was also given a cruel nickname – Gentleman Jack. All because Anne was a lesbian, something about which, considering the time, she was remarkably brazen.

Anne grew up in the West Riding of Yorkshire in a life of financial comfort. Her father was an ex-soldier and minor landowner. She had been born in Halifax in 1791, but the family moved to their small estate when she was still a toddler. The Listers had seven children in all, but only Anne and her sister Marian survived into full adulthood.

Anne was different from the start. In a time when to be a little girl was to be seen but not heard, to be demure and a model of good etiquette, she was a tomboy, a rebellious and rumbustious urchin more akin to a street child from a Dickens' novel than a Regency girl from the borders of high society. She was only seven when her parents, unable to tame her temperament, sent her to a boarding school. There, her high spirits so infuriated her teachers that she was forced to sleep in an attic bedroom, lest she should untowardly influence her peers.

It seems as though Anne's first sexual encounter occurred when she was fifteen. The girl was another whose face did not fit in with the rigid expectations of the school. She was half Indian. And illegitimate. In all likelihood, those in charge would think Eliza Raine should be better employed cleaning up after their students rather than trying to be one of them.

Anne recorded her thoughts in a code of her own making. The sort of strong will that Anne needed to be the person she wanted to be had a downside. Like Dorothy Thomas, Anne could be hard and unsympathetic as she sought to fulfil her dreams. As a fifteen-year-old unhappily boarded out at an unforgiving school, that dream involved becoming extremely rich without having to achieve such good fortune on the back of a man. Eliza would soon inherit a fortune. So while the half-Indian daughter of an English surgeon seems to be fully in love with Anne, the English girl's feelings are more complex. Yes, she is fond of Eliza, and yes, she enjoys the physical side of their relationship. But she is also aware that if she plays her cards right, she may well find herself coming into money.

Yet even this hard business side of Anne cannot compete with her fascination for other women. She meets Mariana Belcombe, and immediately casts Eliza aside. The action destroys Eliza, and she ends up in an asylum. Meanwhile, Anne develops an almost scientific detachment about her feelings. At a time when, according to aspects of public society, lesbianism cannot and does not exist, she knows her own passions. Perhaps what she does not yet understand, however, is that beneath the thin veneer of society's spoken expectations, there is an awareness that some women like other women, just as some men prefer other men. Those feelings exist, but best not to talk about them. Equally, some families will encourage their daughters to embark on lesbian relationships. At least they won't become pregnant and ruin their chances of a good marriage. This hypocrisy and lack of acceptance, have a bad impact on Anne. Unable to express herself as fully as she wishes, she becomes cold and engages in a series of short-lived, physical encounters which satisfy her lust but not her heart.

The feeling, it seems, is mutual. All that prevents the two from becoming a couple is the expectation of society. And that is a big, apparently unsurmountable, barrier. The two travel tens of miles between their northern homes to meet. Then, it has to happen. Mariana marries and claims absolute love for her new husband. It was a custom at the time for a female companion to accompany a new wife on her honeymoon, and that duty falls to Anne. She is horrified by the experience. 'She believed herself or seemed to believe herself, over head and ears in love. Yet she sold her person to another.' Anne records her bitter feelings in her diary, calling the marriage no more than 'legal prostitution'.[30]

Anne continues to involve herself in brief flings with willing women among Yorkshire's social elite, including, incredibly, Mariana's sister. Then once more, Mariana and Anne meet, and their affair begins again. According to Anne, at the behest of her now married former and once more lover.

But the relationship has changed. In an act of romance, Anne once walked ten miles in the Yorkshire rain to intercept Mariana's carriage. The plan was to surprise her. This she did but discovered Mariana with her sister, another passenger and maid. Mariana was furious. For her, their relationship must always remain secret. Later, Mariana told her lover that she was too masculine and that it was embarrassing to be seen with her in public. Anne might have a skin of steel, but it corroded to nothing in the criticism of her true love.

With her love affair broken, Anna travelled to Paris, where she resumed her promiscuous lifestyle. Some relationships lasted longer. Some were shorter, some just a brief encounter. Nothing, though, could replace Mariana. She embarked on ever more adventurous travels, and sometimes Mariana would accompany her. If not Mariana, other women could, easily be found. Following the death of her uncle, she inherited the family estate, which funded her trips and more. It has to be admitted that Anne is a bit of a snob. She looks down her nose at Halifax life but is intrigued by genuine high society. Now her money gives her the opportunity to mix with the elite of the elite. She falls in love again, this time with Vere Hobart, whose brother is the Earl of Buckingham. She attends royal events in Paris and sees the life about which she has dreamed. But Regency times are Regency times. An eminent young woman is expected to marry an equally suitable man, even if she now has some say in who that man will be. What she cannot do is announce that she is a lesbian and engage in a marriage with another woman. So Vere marries, and once more, Anne is heartbroken. But there is a strong character burning in Anne. She returns to her estate at Shibden and sets about renovating its faded charms. Soon she meets an old friend from years before. Ann Walker. Ann has undergone recent tragedies, having lost both her parents and her fiancé.

But the two women with almost identical names are made for each other. After a period of doubt and anxiety, they 'wed' in a simple ceremony (gay marriage being, in those days, not even a consideration), and they set up home together in Shibden. They cause outrage in the local community.

Their marriage was tempestuous at times but also exciting and loving. Anne is the adventurous one, tackling mountains and extremes of weather and conditions. Ann stays by her side, sometimes complaining, always loyal. It is the thrill of adventure that splits them in the end. The two travel to the Caucasus in the far east of Europe. The area is hot, humid and full of mosquitoes. It is there that Anne is bitten, the bite becomes infected, and she dies.

After an eight-month journey back through Europe, coffin at her side, Ann brings her wife back to Shibden, which she now inherits thanks to Anne's will. But her relatives have never come to terms with her love for another woman. 'She must be mad,' they determine. They organise a party to break into Shibden and carry her off to an asylum. The same one which still houses Eliza Raine.

It took another one hundred and fifty years for Anne Lister's diaries to be properly decoded and for the full extent of her feelings, her conquests and her liaisons to be understood. Now a blue plaque, surrounded by a rainbow of circles, looks down from the walls of Holy Trinity Church, York, the place where Anne and Ann were married. She is often called the first lesbian. That is almost certainly not true, but what is the case is that her diaries prove that a woman could, and did, enjoy a love life that was not always heterosexual. For that knowledge alone, the world must be grateful.

The extent to which a person might go to hide their sexuality is illustrated by the case of Eliza Edwards (date of birth unknown, which says a lot), an actress who often used the name Lavinia Walstein. On the face of it, Eliza was a moderately successful actress, best known in Ireland but she also performed in England. She died young, around the age of 24, from lung disease.

Except, most of the above is untrue. So untrue that an inquest into her death created such a cauldron of boiling interest that the police had to be called to keep order. At least, so claimed a journalist from the London Standard. It seems as though her fame as an actress was not great enough for her face to be recognised because her body had been taken to a coroner for dissection, as was the case at the time when a corpse could not be identified. It was when this surgeon examined her that he discovered that the victim was not a woman but a 'perfect man'.

(Although, it seems, not that perfect. While it was determined that some disease of the lungs had killed Eliza, her liver was badly damaged, indicating she was a drunk. She was also found to be much older than claimed, possibly in her mid-forties.)

A witness confirmed that he knew Eliza from many years back, when she would pass as both a man and a woman. That she also lived with several men over time suggests that she was a transgender male, living in secret.

Another contemporary journal reflects public mores. '...one of the most horrible cases of depravity he (the coroner) had ever met with',[31] it declaims with stentorian outrage and prudishness.

Anne Lister and Eliza Edwards experienced the ire of society because of their sexuality. In Eliza's case, it is the exposure of her lifestyle that causes outrage, not the actual existence of it. The same is true, perhaps to a lesser extent, for Anne. After all, it is that she dresses a bit like a man that seems to cause anger among others rather than that she is a woman who hunts female lovers.

Therefore the safest and almost certainly most common approach adopted by lesbian lovers is to present an outward picture of innocent friendship and companionship while, behind the closed curtains, life is lived as these proponents wish it to be lived. The most famous case of this features the Ladies of Llangollen.

We do not know for absolute certainty that Eleanor Butler and Sarah Ponsonby[32] were lovers. Maybe they were just two gentle, ageing women without husbands who sought companionship to ward away loneliness. Maybe. But probably not.

There are plenty of reasons why the ladies may have joined forces. The two upper-class ladies were born in Dublin on the same day. Their own parents died at a similar time, and the two unfortunate orphans were raised together. Perhaps it is inevitable that two children thrown together in such circumstances would grow up to shun the company of others. Sufficiently so that as each reached the age where romance might be expected to blossom, they turned away from the company with which their families wanted them to mix.

So much so that one morning Eleanor and Sarah decide that enough is enough. They head down the coast to Waterford and climb aboard a merchant ship soon to sail. This is an attempt to escape the pressures their families are attempting to put them through, but they do not quite make it and are removed from the ship before it can set off to pastures new, dragged back to their homes and then separated, forcibly, to break the bond of friendship which is now considered to be unhealthy. But sexual? The doubts must surely have existed in the minds of those charged with their protection. If so, they remain unspoken, publicly at least. The two are, though, impossible to keep apart. They once more head to the coast and travel over the Irish Sea to the mountains of North Wales. They head into the green valleys, as far from civilisation as they can be and there find a cottage, almost derelict but private.

They are not alone for long. Back in Ireland, the two had been brought up in the care of a nurse, Mary Carryl. She is distraught that her two charges have fled their homes and determines to follow them, eventually turning up at the still uncomfortable cottage. While the two want their privacy, they welcome their former nurse into the home, and she, in turn, continues to mother them. She helps to provide for them, and when at one stage it seems that they might be evicted, she uses her own savings to buy the cottage for the three of them.

Time passes, and two are buried under a three-sided pyramid, one wall for each bearing an epitaph of that lady's life. Two sides are completed because Mary and Eleanor are already dead. The third wall waits patiently, soon to welcome Sarah Ponsonby.

The story is romantic, archetypically Regency and, unsurprisingly, complete rubbish. Actually, not total nonsense because some facts are true, or just minor distortions of the truth, but the overall mood of the piece? Misleading. Well-meant. Yet wrong. But how else, in 1830, to explain the lives of women whose relationship could not be honestly reported? Hence, the Freemans Journal of that year reports the couple's life stories. Thus these are lives that cannot be ignored because the women's home has become such a social hub for leading characters of the day that it turns the twin hostesses into significant personalities of their time. But equally, their lives cannot be reported truthfully. Not when they are lived by ladies of class.

So to the truth. The couple meet when Eleanor is 29 and Sarah, a girl sixteen years her junior. Sarah has just been enrolled in her boarding school and is an orphan (Eleanor is not). When her carers, her first cousin once removed Lady Betty Fownes and her husband, are away, Eleanor steps in as a guardian. The next stage of their journey together is closer to the Freemans Journal report – they develop an intense friendship, albeit one that at some stage becomes sexual and then, after ten years together, they elope to Wales, certainly without their parents' or guardians' support. Further, Mary also exists and does journey along with her ladies.

There are similarities between the Ladies of Llangollen and Anne Lister. They, too, dress in a masculine way and are open enough about their relationship for friends to refer to the older Eleanor using masculine pronouns. Equally, it appears that they do not hide their affection for each other. They use tender endearments towards one another: 'my dear', 'my beloved' and so forth, and as with Anne and Ann, regard themselves as a married couple.

It does seem as though it was not that unusual for ladies to form such close bonds that they would decide to set up home together and consider themselves as a couple. However, where we are much less certain is the extent to which these relationships became sexual. Mostly because to be so open about such matters was, at best, to risk the scorn of society, at worst, to end up before the courts. From today's perspective, we can easily assume that such relationships were sexual. Yet there is a 'but'… social pressure is an extremely powerful control on behaviour, and perhaps it was of sufficient strength to prevent a relationship between two women from reaching sexual proportions.

Two ladies of upper-class backgrounds inhabiting a quiet, secluded cottage in the Welsh countryside is unusual enough to provoke the interests of libertine Regency types. The Ladies of Llangollen are frequently hosts to the more Avant Garde elements of that society. Wordsworth, Lord Byron and even, surprisingly perhaps, the Duke of Wellington become occasional guests at their home. Often, people of note might ask to drop by without notice – the ladies are often, but not always, happy to receive them.

It is easy to see why two such characters lit flames of interest in the general public. They would appear about town in top hats; they would dress identically. They were larger than life but also private. Eleanor and Sarah lived in the cottage, which was sin Plas Newydd, for half a century. It seems as though, unlike so many women of that time, they eventually lived the lives they wanted for themselves.

We cannot get away from the question as to whether that life included sex. It is hard to believe it did not, which in turn makes it equally hard to believe that other women did not share equally close, loving, physical, but secretive relationships at the same time. Even if often they were hidden behind the screen of 'companionship' or even a heterosexual marriage.

It is often said that the reason we know so little about lesbians of the Regency era is because, to all intents and purposes, public perception of the era is that such a sexuality does not exist. What we can conclude is that this is only partly true. Surely people are aware of lesbianism. It just suits them to pretend that they are not.

CHAPTER 9

BEHIND CLOSED DOORS: NOT SO SECRET AFFAIRS

We began our perusal of the Regency with matters of the heart, and it would be wrong to end without a return to the romantic and salacious. To indulge in any kind of affair during the period might evoke much tutting and head shaking, but only in public. Behind the scenes, such liaisons are part and parcel of the times. As we saw in the previous chapter, even a dalliance with the same sex is OK as long as it is not too overt. Similarly, a menage a trois will elicit no more than a knowing nod provided a man is not seen publicly engaging in hanky panky, a lady on each arm. These are times of growing openness and tolerance. Of a sort. There are some conditions to be met. An attempt to keep any untoward relationship quiet is the first and foremost requirement to keep one's peers happy.

We might call it hypocrisy these days or even dishonesty. In Regency times, outward appearances are all. Nobody is too fussed about what occurs behind the heavy velvet curtains. Inevitably, though, greater expectations of propriety are placed upon the woman compared to the man. Ideally, she should have married first before embarking on some Regency rumpty-tumpty. Out of respect to her husband, she should have provided him with an heir. Then, with these conditions met, she is free to be wooed by a man of means. Ideally, an older one, but such a requirement is not set in stone.

Religion is important in the period, and a tenet of the bible is that one should not commit adultery. How to resolve the conflict between this commandment and the fun of a little extra-marital fling? There are many reasons which combine to paint a layer of respectability over a dishonourable act, and perhaps the heaviest hue comes from the point that some of the most ardent participants in unsanctioned coitus are society's leading figures. It is yet another oxymoron of the Regency period that while, maybe for the first time in history, it is seen as totally acceptable to lampoon those in power, they also wield as much social influence as ever. In fact, the growth of newspapers and periodicals is thanks to improved printing and distribution methods. It could be argued that their influence is now the greatest it has ever been, at least to date.

Perhaps that is a matter of convenience. Both men and women enjoy illicit relationships. It provides a defence against morally dubious behaviour. Whatever, it is useful for others that two of the most openly proliferate sexual beings of that confusing, remarkable era are the head of society himself and the man whose cultural influence is the greatest of his time. Those are, of course, the Regent, the future George IV, Prince of Wales and the incorrigible lover, poet, commentator and all-round rogue, Lord Byron.

Let us start with the latter and take a look at some of the most significant partners in which the not-so-good Lord initially romanced and then abandoned. First and foremost among these is most probably Lady Caroline Lamb, who coined the phrase 'mad, bad and dangerous to know', when talking of her sometime lover. The two met in 1812 when Lady Caroline was twenty-seven, three years older than her predatory partner. She met the criteria to embark on an affair. Both the conventional ones and the ones of the heart. She was married and had produced a son for her husband. At the same time, her own marriage was struggling. Her husband is William Lamb, who is the younger son of Lord and Lady Melbourne, whom, in turn, Byron lists among his closest friends. Lady Melbourne is a mother figure to the wayward poet, a confidante and a supporter of him. It is through the Melbourne family that Lady Caroline and Byron meet. At the time, William is more interested in his political career than his wife, and their young son suffers from medical problems. He is also most probably autistic. Perhaps worst of all, William plays the field wantonly and engages in sexual fetishes that disturb Lady Caroline.

When Lady Caroline and Byron finally meet, it is she who is first attracted. Byron likes a conquest, but she offers no barriers to romance. Lady Caroline is immediately enchanted by him, he much less so by her, for the reason above. Further, she does not possess the typical looks considered attractive at the time. She is tall and thin and dresses a little eccentrically, almost boyishly in a way, as though she is still a child. Meanwhile, Lady Caroline notes: 'That beautiful pale face is my fate.'[33]

However, as they begin to know each other better, Caroline's attractions start to play their magic on Byron. He learns that it is not just physicality that engages him, and in Caroline, he sees someone whose complete disregard for the opinions of others fascinates him. Yet, at the same time, he is uncomfortable with her flirtatiousness. Byron's excessive womanising is believed now to be a reaction to a fundamental insecurity as though by seducing a reluctant or hard-to-obtain woman, he could bolster his own ego. There is no thrill in hunting a caged animal. (In fact, today, most of us will also claim that there is no fun either in hunting a wild animal. The so-called sport still takes place, though.) He does not know how to cope with a lady whose infatuation with him is something on which he does not have to work.

Yet, conversely, he finds this confusion stimulating and is besotted with a passion he struggles to rationalise. That, too, in turn, heightens his attraction to this woman. Their affair flourishes and is sufficiently open to shock London society. Or, at least, induce in it an appearance of scandalisation. Meanwhile, the affair is intense, both in the passion of their love and the fury of their disagreements. They are different characters – Caroline loves to dance and enjoy herself; Byron, who suffers from a club foot, can only sit and watch others party. She is sympathetic, however, and often sits with him as they watch other couples waltz the room.

She is also an intellectual equal to Byron, which is an eye opener for him. There is a vein of misogyny running through the poet that tells him a man is intellectually superior to an equivalent woman. He discovers in Caroline that this is not true, and to be fair to him, he learns from this. She feels sufficiently attached to him to offer her jewels so he may pawn them for money – he is regularly short of the means required to meet the lifestyle for which he craves. Yet, at the same time, Caroline is overtly fond of her husband William for all his manifold faults. Byron, equally, cannot keep his eyes and hands off other women. Each position is a source of constant tension between the two, and frequently this erupts into volcanic fury from one or both.

Today, we might be able to analyse Byron's character with greater accuracy and determine in him a flaw - a mental condition – which explains his wanton desire for women and then his inability to keep them. On the one hand, he needs them to love him unreservedly. On the other, he finds the thrill of the chase to be what keeps his interest. Thus every relationship is doomed to fail, and this one is no different. But, for Byron at least, it comes closer to enduring than most. In May 1812, only a couple of months into their affair, he suggests that they flee England. In all likelihood, he does not mean it. Caroline refuses to state that she loves him more than William, a stance that both infuriates him and arouses him. But the extreme emotions that each of them feels means that their relationship is both visible to the public and highly charged. It is worth stating again that people have no problem with an affair, provided they do not know about it. This one is as public as a headline in a newspaper, and that angers society. Byron is persuaded to leave London.

Yet this complex relationship has so many layers to unravel. Lady Caroline will not commit herself to Byron but is equally distraught that he has left her. She writes, and he does not reply. He returns to London, is persuaded to leave again, and plans to head for Harrow. The small town, then only a few miles from London (now subsumed within it), is easily reachable from Caroline's abode at Melbourne House, and she determines to visit. A young, married woman openly visiting another man's home, unaccompanied. Society will convulse. No problem that the two are sleeping together because that is behind closed doors. What must not happen is for the lady to be witnessed passing through that door. Caroline, though, is beyond caring. She is infatuated with Byron, and now he is ignoring her. She disguises herself badly and arrives at his London home. Apparently, such is the shock that a crowd gathers to witness the event. (This may be an example of hyperbole – the information comes from the diary of a friend.)[34] This friend, Hobhouse, tells her to leave. She seizes a knife and attempts to stab herself.

How serious the attempted suicide might be, we do not know, but she fails. It is enough to persuade Byron to write to her later, urging her not to kill herself. William, meanwhile, seems relatively unperturbed by the whole sordid shenanigans. He is holidaying at his country home and intending to travel to Ireland. His father urges Caroline to go with him, an idea about which William seems surprisingly (or not, given the public nature of her affair) ambivalent. In the end, she goes, but only because Byron advises that she should.

Once apart, passions cool, and the affair – a lifetime of craving in the shortest of time spans – ends. But Caroline's infatuation does not. She can never come to terms with his rejection of her. Today, we would explain her behaviour as a kind of emotional breakdown. London society, though, is relatively small and incestuous (a word particularly apt when applied near to the name Byron). The two meet at various events. There is a formality and coldness between them now, which still occasionally erupts into violence. Strong words are exchanged at a dance when Caroline attempts to wind up her former lover about his clubbed foot. His sarcastic reply means she grabs a knife, and as her friends remove it, she cuts herself. That story makes the papers.

At another time, she enters his home when he is away and scrawls graffiti on his books. But it is not all one-sided. Within a year of their separation, Byron embarks on an affair with the self-styled Countess of Oxford, who just happens to be – or has been – a close friend of Caroline. While the relationship is public knowledge, he cruelly tells Caroline that he has given his heart to another but cannot name her. It is as though, having wooed her, loved her and then abandoned her, Byron is now sticking needles in her heart.

It does seem the case that his affair with Jane Harley (1774-1824), the same Countess of Oxford, was a brief meeting of equally flagrant bed hoppers. Harley was an important figure in the movement for reform, but the daughter of a vicar would equally have made the perfect subject for a Ray Cooney farce. So rampant was her willingness to embark on affairs that her fourteen children were commonly referred to as the Harleian Miscellany because nobody knew which lover might be their father. Commentators of that day do love a dabble in satire. What did seem fairly certain was that none of that particular miscellany was a child created from her loveless relationship with her husband, Edward Harley, who was both the Earl of Oxford and Earl Mortimer.

But while it does seem as though Byron could be heartlessly cruel to Caroline, on other occasions, there seems to be some kind of affection between them. Close to the end of his own life, Byron thanks her for her loyalty, recognising that although he is widely despised, she has always loved him. According to Caroline, their final meeting ends with a gentle kiss. Although, that may just be a bit of poetic licence.

As for Caroline, she is changed forever by the affair. She pens some novels, attempts to rebuild her relationship with William, and goes through life. But she is an anaemic version of the woman she once was. In the end, she and William separate. Yet something remains between them, and it is William who is by her bedside when she dies in 1828.

Not every relationship into which the poet flung himself led to quite such outrageous consequences. In 1811, the year before he embarked on the life-changing dalliance with Lady Caroline, he had met Lady Frances Webster. Frances was born in 1793, and now she is the wife of a close friend of Byron, James Webster. Not that being a mate is much of a deterrent to stop Byron from cuckolding a fellow peer. He persuades himself that their marriage is one of convenience and sets off for a gathering at the Yorkshire-located Aston Hall, where Webster and Frances live.

Coldly, Byron's intent behind the journey north is purely to seduce Frances – another notch on his scabby bedpost. However, he does not succeed. Apparently, according to one of his many letters to Lady Melbourne, he notes with some surprise that Frances turns down his advances. Later, they share some notes but nothing more. Byron explains his failure by claiming that Frances is attracted to a different man, her husband's solicitor. Possibly this is the case, although there does not seem to be conclusive evidence of such. Hard as it might be for someone such as Byron to take, possibly Frances Webster just did not find him attractive, and was, in any case, happily enough married to feel that embarking on an affair was just something she did not want to do, however much an ego as great as Byron's might find such a set of circumstances hard to bear.

We have already talked about Mary Shelley and know of the close relationship between her husband and Byron. Her stepsister, too, came under the spell of the rogue poet. This time, with very notable results. Claire Mary Jane Clairmont was born in 1798 and is the sister who is the favourite of Shelley's stepmother. Perhaps, as her own biological daughter, that is understandable. As hard as it was for Mary to see her stepsister treated so favourably compared to herself, it did not stop the two from becoming close.

The identity of Claire's father remained secret during her life. Indeed, it was not until research in 2010 revealed his name that it became apparent he was the Baronet of Sandhill Park, one John Lethbridge. We have already gained some insight into Claire's life growing up as a child – certainly, it was less oppressive than her stepsister Mary's. She first sees her future lover in 1812 when both are at a lecture on Shakespeare given by another well-known poet, Samuel Taylor Coleridge. Her stepfather certainly enjoyed some good connections as a mentor to this array of budding romantic poets. Conveniently for them, this group of young men were advocates of free love. There is a more than reasonable chance that Claire had enjoyed a physical relationship with Shelley before Byron.

As Mary's and Shelley's love blossomed and retreated, Claire accompanied them. They moved around London to various abodes as a three – rather than a threesome, it is assumed. Before in 1815, Claire sets out for the North Devon coast at Lynmouth, there to enjoy the picturesque, one presumes. Although her mother no doubt had a part in this decision, reluctant as she is to see her biological daughter remain so close to a couple about whom she disapproves. Soon she is back with her stepsister and her husband, and the three now travel to Europe. Their first stop is Geneva, and it is on this trip that the ghost storytelling occurs, which inspires Mary Shelley to write 'Frankenstein'.

It is in Europe, we believe, that Claire falls under Byron's spell, albeit not for long. She becomes pregnant, travels back to England and gives birth to a daughter, Allegra. This is, appropriately enough for the period, in the Regency city of Bath. Now comes the hardest decision of Claire's life; it is a sign of the times that she makes a call she will regret, a shocking one, but one she feels she cannot avoid. A young unmarried mother of some social standing cannot be seen with a baby. She agrees to place the child in her father's care. She feels that Allegra's life chances will be better with Byron than with herself. It seems as though Byron is a reasonable enough father to the girl. However, when she is just four or so, he travels with her to Italy and stays with Countess Teresa Guiccioli. A woman who, surprise, surprise, becomes his lover, albeit his final one.

The countess' husband is forty years her senior. However, the rampant Lord is still afraid of how he may react to their romance. As is often the case, Byron has caused outrage not only by conducting the affair but especially for doing so openly and brazenly. It seems as though sensibilities in Italy were not too different to those in England at the time. According to reports, Byron walked around constantly armed with pistols and a sword, lest the Count should seek revenge for the humiliation the poet had bestowed upon him.

It is thought that this relationship had begun as far back as 1818, and it was in 1821 that Byron returned to the idyllic city of Ravenna on the Adriatic Coast, not far from the romantic Venice. This time he has Allegra in tow, and it seems that the reason for his visit may be two-fold. Both to see Teresa and to hand his daughter, remember just four years old, to the nuns at the convent of S. Giovanni in nearby Bagnacavallo. At the time, the convent-educated daughters of the elite, although to place the girl in their care at the tender age of four seems excessive even for those times.

Later, Shelley's family would visit the small girl and report that she was doing well. However, she died the following year. Even among the highest echelons of society, childhood mortality was an unfortunate fact of life. Or death. Reportedly, Claire would never forgive Byron for what happened, even though he can only carry the blame for the decision to send Allegra to the convent, not for the fact that there she caught an illness and died.

Following Shelley's accidental death, it appears that Mary and Claire drifted apart. Mary concentrated on her commitments to improve society, and Claire took a number of jobs as a Governess around Europe. Claire was fluent in a number of languages, and it was this that kept poverty from her door. Later she returned to England and worked as a music teacher whilst looking after her ailing mother. Then, in 1844, life takes a turn for the better. Financially at least. Percy Bysshe Shelley's father dies, and perhaps a little surprisingly, it transpires that he has settled a sizeable benefit on Claire. Suddenly she has an income of £12000 per year. She moves to Florence and into her dotage, where maybe dementia sets in. She is described as becoming increasingly eccentric.

She dies in 1879. Claire's is a sad life. Maybe her flirtation with Byron has proved to be life-defining, both for the affair itself and the consequences for Allegra. She never marries and, it seems, never again finds love – if indeed love was what existed between Byron and herself all those years ago.

Meanwhile, what of Teresa Guiccioli? Teresa lived from 1800 to 1873, and maybe Byron had been wise to carry arms while in Ravenna. Her husband, the Count, was a notorious character. He may be old, but he was certainly opportunistic and cutthroat, with loyalty only to himself. Apparently a supporter of the Pope, he defected to Napoleon when it seemed beneficial to do so. Only to abandon the emperor when his own fortunes failed. He may not have been too pleased either that his wife's affair with Byron began only three days after their wedding.

In fact, unusually, as far as Byron's relationships went, and the one he enjoyed with his actual wife is included here, it seems as though genuine love existed between himself and Teresa. From the point she posted him a cutting of her pubic hair (an Italian tradition, apparently, which indicates a willingness to embark on an affair) to his death, there is real and lasting affection between them, despite the danger of the Count deciding to end their relationship… violently.

Northern Italy at the time was an uncertain place. Teresa's father, Count Gamba, was a nationalist who sought to unify the country and remove the region from being under the thumb of the Austrian Empire. Consequentially, he was exiled and only allowed to return on the understanding that Byron end his relationship with Teresa and she returns to her husband's side. It may have been the thought that their affair must end that ultimately led Byron to board the Hercules, the ship on which he was to travel to Greece, where, shortly after, he would succumb to a fever and die.

Teresa was heartbroken that the man with whom she had lived as a common law wife for five years was leaving and was inconsolable as the ship left the harbour. Her brother, too, travelled with her lover to the warring nation.

She did marry again, this time giving her consent to the Marquis de Boissy. However, this may well have been a marriage of convenience rather than love. The Marquis seemed more interested in her relationship with Byron than his wife herself, boasting that he had married the poet and playboy's former lover.

There is a poignant footnote to Teresa's life. The childless woman who found love with a wayward poet and maybe even tamed him wrote two manuscripts about the paramour she described as 'the king of men'. These papers were discovered after her death and then hidden away in her family's archives. They were afraid that Teresa's relationship could bring shame on the family name. Only after they were rediscovered in 2005 were the stories of her relationship with her one true love published.

If Lord Byron was a leading playboy of the times, then his position at the top of that dubious league table is severely challenged by society's most prominent figure, the Prince of Wales. One whose promiscuity began when he was little more than a child, who married in a drunken stupor and who loved with a hunger that was both astonishingly intense and, usually, extremely short-lived.

In his defence (albeit a desperate one), by all accounts, he never wished to marry Caroline of Brunswick. Not least, we know his attraction to older women, and Caroline, born in 1768, was six years his junior. The Regent was a man of passion, one whose habit of falling fervently, uncontrollably in love made him a bit of a laughing stock. Unfortunately, such feelings of attraction never arose towards Caroline, which is hardly surprising. It is not just that, in the good looks stakes, she had little going for her. Looks might initially attract a partner of either gender, but usually, it is a person's character and personality that sets up a romance. But there are limits. Although, it seems, not for Caroline. Cleanliness was, for example, something to which she paid little attention. While it is not especially clear how reliable such reports might be, she apparently rarely changed her undergarments, while even more widely known among her acquaintances (the evidence being self-explanatory) was her foul body odour. On embracing her just prior to their wedding, the Regent is reported to have staggered away nauseated and then drunk brandy for three days solid to numb him from the horror of what he was about to do. Supposedly he was so drunk on the day of his wedding that he collapsed into a royal grate and did not move until the following dawn.

Mind you, they did conceive Princess Charlotte. After a year of marriage, the Prince decided enough was enough and promptly wrote to her to tell her that she could do as she liked. Still, he had no intention of living with her any longer; certainly, any prospect of intimacy was well off the cards. This is from a man for whom lust seems a primary instinct. It begs the question as to why the two got together in the first place. From Caroline's perspective, the answer is clear – who would not turn down the chance to become a Queen, even if she would have to wait a while? For the Prince of Wales, the answer is equally easy to reach. The Brunswick line is extremely rich and the Prince of Wales is not. In fact, he is in debt to the tune of £630000, an embarrassingly high figure at any time in history, but in 1795 an absolute fortune. Parliament is clear – the heir to the throne must provide an heir of his own and, at the same time, strengthen political links by selecting a German bride. Do that, they tell the wayward prince, and they will settle his debts. This really is a time when relations between the monarchy and Parliament are at one of their lowest ebbs.

On receiving the note telling her, not that politely, to go away, Caroline does just that. She heads to Blackheath and there establishes a lifestyle of worrying sexual deviancy. During a time when for a lady to raise a glimmer of a smile at the wrong time is to commit social hari-kari, Caroline's habit of dancing semi-naked in front of guests is unthinkably crude. She keeps a clockwork figure which performs sexual gestures and, as far back as 1806, she is thought to have had an illegitimate son fathered by a footman. Lady Chatterley, eat your heart out. A royal commission is set up to investigate, called with wonderful understatement the 'Delicate Investigation'. But as much as with political enquiries today, this investigation is primarily designed to quieten outrage, and no conclusions are reached.

Among her other improprieties, Caroline is said to have become the mistress of King Joachim, who was Napoleon's brother-in-law. It is hard to think of a liaison more provocative to a regent who regards the French Emperor as his sworn enemy. Mind you, it is hard to see what might have inspired King Joachim's attraction towards her, unless it was to wind up the English monarchy. Or, maybe later in life, she had begun to take baths. It could be that this is the answer because she is also accused of taking her ablutions together with another lover, one Bartolomeo Bergami. She performed her bathing in front of servants seems an unnecessary extra detail about a lady who wandered around her court topless and danced naked to the waist at a high society Geneva ball.

At one point, the Government tried to get the marriage annulled, the House of Lords taking the unusual step of bringing her forwards before it. The grounds for this strange manoeuvre was none other than her affair with the aforementioned 'foreigner'. Dancing naked, it seems, one could get away with. But have relations with a low-browed foreigner, and the world caves in.

Still, that attempt failed, as did the offer of a bribe of £50000 if Caroline would agree to stay out of the country.

Following George III's death in January 1820, the Regent became King. Which, painfully and bizarrely, meant Caroline of Brunswick was Queen. Except isn't there always a 'but' when it comes to the Regency? At a time when the upper classes lived in a way completely out of touch with ordinary people, there was a ground roots fondness for Caroline of Brunswick. George III was unpopular and mad. The Regent was unpopular and lampooned. Caroline had an earthy quality to which the general public warmed. She was one of them (if not in the background), and that angered those in Parliament and the aristocracy at least as much as her behaviour. Painfully and bizarrely, she became Queen. Yes, but not to most, only to the few, albeit the few who wielded most power.

George IV was crowned in July 1821; his estranged wife was not invited. When she arrived at the door of Westminster Abbey and demanded to be allowed in, she was at first admitted and then almost as quickly locked out. Distraught, she left, demanding a coronation of her own. It was not to be forthcoming, and three weeks later, she fell ill and died. Painfully. And bizarrely.

The question is begged whether the two should ever have been allowed to marry in the first place. Because possibly, maybe, the Prince of Wales is already married. But not to the right person. Just somebody he loved. There are not many reasons to be sympathetic towards George, but this may be one of the few.

Maria Fitzherbert was born in Shropshire in 1756. And that is about as much as is known about her as a young child, apart from the fact that her family name is Smythe and she has only the loosest, most tenuous ties to any kind of aristocracy. Oh, and one more important point. She is a Catholic. And that is a problem. If anybody can be said to be unfortunate in love, it is Maria. Firstly she marries a somewhat senior gentleman, Edward Weld. Whether that is for love or for money, history does not reveal. Certainly, Edward is extremely comfortably off. It seems as though the excitement of hitching himself to the attractive young Maria, though, is an adventure too far. Within three months of their wedding day, he dies, and to add particularly strong sea salt to the weeping wounds of Maria, he leaves her nothing in his will.

Next, she marries Thomas Fitzherbert. Together they have a son, who dies, and four years after their wedding, Thomas also passes away in Nice. Still, at least financially, she is comfortable now. Thomas leaves her a regular income and a London townhouse. The two-time widow makes her way back to London, stopping off for a while in Paris. It is while she is attending an opera in the English capital that another, somewhat more famous, member of the audience spots her. The passionate Prince is immediately entranced and seeks to turn Maria into yet another mistress. She is made of sterner stuff. It seems as though there is some attraction to the Regent rampant, but she knows that as a catholic and a twice-married woman, marriage is not going to be on the cards. At the same time, she does not wish to become just another in a long line of mistresses on the arm of a wayward and immature future monarch. George is just 22 at this time.

Technically, marriage is a possibility. It is certainly something George suggests as his attempts to woo Maria as his mistresses are rejected one by one. But three matters stand in the way. Firstly, the law. The Royal

Marriages Act and the Act of Settlement combine to mean that should any in line for the monarchy marry a Catholic, they must forgo their right to the throne. That might not have been too much of a problem were George not next in line. But he is. The benefits of the monarchy or the benefits of a wife? It is not too tough a call. Love conquers all, and surely he feels it best to act now and sort out the consequences later. Although to be fair, he is faced with the second more intransigent problem as well. At 22, he is too young to marry without his father's permission, and that will not be granted if his proposed wife is a Catholic. Then there is the third issue. The toughest one of all. Maria refuses to marry him.

George tries every ruse in the book to persuade Maria into his arms, even staging a suicide attempt. Finally, maybe persuaded by the thought that she might go down in history as the woman who caused a king in waiting to kill himself, Maria relents and agrees to the marriage. Having made the commitment, she immediately flees to Europe. The engagement, if that is not too strong a word – it probably is – seems to have a detrimental impact on both. Maria, a lady known for her charm and pleasant spirits, becomes unpredictable and pompous. George, ever more frequently drunk and lecherous. It is not a good image for the next in line to the throne, a position which will soon become even more important given whatever illness it is from which he suffers will shortly begin to affect his father.

But if George is anything, it is stubborn. Once love has again become the foremost influence on the colour of his blood, it is all-consuming. Thanks to a large bribe from the already indebted prince, a clergyman is found who will conduct the wedding, and it takes place, not in a

Cathedral, Abbey, or even a church, but in the drawing room of Maria's London townhouse. The marriage is meant to be a secret, but the two appear together everywhere – George stipulates as much – and those that do not know for sure about the illegal marriage – there are a few - still believe it to have taken place.

But marriage does have a positive effect on the man who may not now become king. He establishes a base in Brighton and puts his wife in a nearby villa. He is cheerier, less prone to drunkenness, spends more wisely and cuts back on his gambling. Maria, it seems, is the sort of woman George has needed for a while. But Parliament is not happy. On the one hand, it recognises that the problem prince is calmer thanks to Maria. On the other, he still carries a huge debt. For George, the main priority is that Parliament covers up both his debt and his marriage. Parliament undertaking a cover-up? Not much changes. However, this plan angers Maria to such an extent that she refuses to see George, believing that in seeking that suppression, he has damaged her reputation.

Around two years into their marriage, in 1788, the problem which prompted a Regency in the first place raises its head. George III experiences his first bout of madness. Whether this is a disease, a reaction to the death of two of his youngest children or has some other cause, doctors are flummoxed. Suddenly, the question of the next in line to the throne being married to a Catholic becomes ever more urgent. The Prince of Wales, ever the opportunist, meanwhile takes the chance to promote his own case for a greater allowance. Publicly, such a move goes down like an unexpected visit from the taxman. He is booed and jeered, and the lampooning press have a field day.

Is it entitlement that blinds the prince to the public's perception of him? George seems incapable of seeing how his behaviour is regarded. As his popularity declines to impossibly low levels, he responds by falling back into drunkenness and engaging in ever more affairs, making hardly an effort to conceal them. He does not care how he is regarded, it seems. There are few times in history when the British Monarchy has been held in lower regard. It is Princess Diana magnified a hundredfold. It might be that George is simply a despicable person, or it could be that his tough upbringing has weakened his spirit so that under any kind of pressure, he relapses. Drunkenness, gambling, womanising. As his relationship with Maria begins to fail, he takes up with another woman, the Countess of Jersey, Frances Villiers. Yet he still thinks that Maria should remain at his side. And that he should not give up his right to the throne. If ever a person wanted their cake, wanted to eat it, cream and all, and then felt they should have a second portion, it is the Prince of Wales.

Yet he does maybe have, deep down, a couple of redeeming features. Sometimes honesty comes to the surface. His marriage is over, and as the prospect of becoming wed to the unwanted Caroline of Brunswick comes closer, he ensures that Maria is looked after financially and states – even on his wedding day – that she is the only woman he will ever truly love. So, it is possible that there is some romance there, after all. Much later, he writes his will and leaves whatever fortune remains to Maria and asks to be buried with a picture of her.

Then Maria is taken ill – seriously so. The effect on George is dramatic. He has a nervous breakdown and begs her not to die. In 1799, the marriage to Caroline of Brunswick over in all but name, the

Pope becomes involved. Remarkably, he decrees that the marriage between Maria and George is acceptable in the eyes of his church at least, and Maria can once more return to live with the man who will, thanks to his father's rapid decline in health, soon become Regent.

But George doesn't really change. He continues to permit himself affairs, and after eight or nine years, Maria has finally had enough. She leaves. Two years on, and George is officially made Regent. His daughter has died by now, and his brothers are positioning themselves to take the throne, marrying any available German Princess who might further their bid.

The true, selfish, self-serving, blindfolded George is meanwhile to the fore. He claims that the marriage was always Maria's idea, and he only agreed out of kindness to her. He is the noble victim here, pilloried for acting altruistically. That is nonsense. His own letters – which she kept – prove it. But there is one last twist. Albeit it takes a long time to arrive. In 1830 George is dying. He receives a letter. It is from Maria. Although he is by now too weak to reply, he is overjoyed to receive it and keeps it under his pillow until he dies. Then, as he is lowered into his coffin, a picture is placed around his neck. It is of his Maria. He gets his wish to be buried with an image of possibly the only woman he ever genuinely loved.

As for Maria, she goes to George's brother, William IV, and puts the record straight before the new king. She shows the letters George has sent to her and tells her story. Fearing that she is after exposing the family, William offers a title, but she does not want it. All that Maria requires is permission to dress as a widow and fit out her servants in royal livery. That permission is granted, and Maria spends her final seven years in mourning, living once more in Brighton. Maria Fitzherbert does not always act in the best way possible, but she is honourable and, considering the hell George puts her through, remarkably loyal and forgiving. It is hard to imagine that, in those last moments of his life, George does not realise the opportunity he has thrown away.

What of the above-mentioned Countess, Frances Villiers? Certainly, of the many women with whom the Prince of Wales fell permanently, irredeemably, passionately in love for eternity, she lasted longer than most. In fact, the Villiers family might seem perfectly matched to the personality of George. Debauchery was in their blood.

Frances was born in 1753 and married into the Villiers family, joining in matrimony to George Bussy Villiers in 1770. She came from appropriately clerical stock. Her father was the Reverend Phillip of Twysden, Bishop of Raphoe. A fine pedigree from which the then seventeen-year-old emerged. Or not. Because the good Reverend was a bit of a rogue, he had been shot dead while engaged in robbing a stagecoach. No doubt, his sermons were interesting to behold.

This is not to suggest that Frances was in any way wayward herself. She produced ten, maybe more, children between 1771 and 1778, and some commentators think that one or two might even have been fathered by her husband. As can be seen, loyalty lay deep within her corpuscles; her best friend is the Duchess of Devonshire, which of course, meant that one of her affairs should be with the duke himself.

Frances first attracted the easily swayed attention of the prince when he was just twenty. It says a lot about what the young man must have been like that Frances chose to pour iced water on his amour back then. Ten years on, she was much more open to his drunken advances. In fact, she was one of the leading reasons he chose to marry Caroline of Brunswick. Not because such a liaison would help the future king sort out his problems, rather that she realised quickly there was no opportunity of the marriage being a success, which could open the way to her own furtherment. Not least, by persuading him to abandon Mary Fitzherbert. As we can see, Frances is a delightful character.

But as well as being hard-nosed and opportunist, she is clever, and she is good company, albeit in a rather dangerous way. A sort of female Lord Byron, in fact. Frances manages to secure the position of Lady of the Bedchamber to Princess Caroline, which gives her considerable influence over the odorous German, and when Caroline takes up George's invitation to leave the Palace, Frances takes over the prince's affairs instead. Affairs, perhaps, being something of an ambiguity in her case.

Their real affair lasted for six years, a time during which her unpopularity exceeded even that of her lover. She is believed to have stolen private letters from the Princess and passed them on to Queen Charlotte – the public perception of her as a meddling chancer is enough for her to have to seek safety at various points during her relationship with George.

We might have got to know a little bit more about this woman, except that upon her death in the summer of 1821, the executor of her will,

Lord Clarendon, was given clear instruction from above. Burn her papers, and especially anything relating to her relationship with the new King, which he did. In turn, that gives us a good clue as to the content of those letters. While we don't know the details, it is a fair conclusion that they would not portray his character in a particularly good light.

Many of the Prince's women could be said to have been defined in history by their relationship to him. That is perhaps inevitable, given his position and his reputation. At least one, though, enjoyed a life so full that her affair with George forms only a footnote to her life. That is Grace Elliot, born in Edinburgh in 1754. The lady who would become, amongst other things, a spy, a best-selling author and mother of a Prince's child. Her father was an army captain and also the Attorney General of Grenada. Grace moved in high circles. She was sent to France to attend a convent school, and the young lady who returned moved in with her father. He and her mother had separated when she was young.

She was just sixteen when an older and extremely wealthy doctor, John Elliot, fell in love with her. They were married, and Grace moved to London, becoming a key member of that society. It was there that she met Lord Valentia, had an affair with him and was divorced by John Elliot. It was clearly an acrimonious event. Elliot won the modern equivalent of £2 million from Valentia for 'criminal conversation', and Grace added a second 't' to her surname in an attempt to separate herself from her former husband.

Grace was sent to another convent in France to atone for her misdemeanours but quickly met Lord Cholmondeley, who took her as his mistress, giving her access back into the London society she craved. Gainsborough even painted her.

It appears, however, that Grace really could not resist the amorous advances of men. It is around this time that she embarks on an affair with the Prince of Wales and then, in 1782, gives birth to a daughter. The prince accepts responsibility for being the father of young Georgiana, but there is a problem. So do three other men. These are Lord Cholmondeley and two gentlemen, respectively, named Charles Wyndham and George Selwyn. In the end, it is the Lord who brings up the child, changing her name to Georgina Seymour.

Two years on, and relations with the prince are still active in some respects at least. He introduces Grace to the Duc D'Orleans. It does not take long before she is ensconced in a splendid Paris home with a hearty income from her latest lover. Then the French Revolution rather spoils her life. Her lover declares support for the revolutionaries, but that does not save him from the guillotine. He becomes a victim of the 1793 Reign of Terror. Grace rather bravely remains in France and acts as a spy for the British whilst simultaneously seeking to protect the French aristocrats with whom she has been mixing. She even hides one between her mattresses while she lies on her bed, pretending to be ill. This is one of the stories in her best-selling account of the revolution, 'Journal of My Life During the French Revolution'. The book is published posthumously.

The revolutionaries catch up with Grace in the end. She is imprisoned but escapes execution. Eventually, she is sent back to England. Then, remarkably she returns to France when Napoleon comes to power. Rumours are that he wishes to take her as his mistress, although, as by now, Grace is a mature woman, this may not be true.[35] Her final affair is with the Mayor of Ville-d'Avray, and she lives with him to the west of Paris, enjoying a life of comfort. Grace dies in 1823 but remains a figure of interest. A film was made of her life in 2001, and she frequently appears in books about the Regency and the Revolution.

The Prince of Wales's affairs are too numerous to cover all. Indeed, it is likely he engaged in many short-lived dalliances which are not recorded. Even as a youth, he seemed unable to resist sex, often with mature women as his partner. Maybe that is because Prince George's first mistress was the much older Mary Robinson.

By the time she came to the attention of the young prince, Mary was a reasonably well-known actress and poet. She was born in 1757 and suffered an early lesson about the infidelity of men. Her father left them, leaving her mother to bring up her five children. Hester Vanacott, though, was a resourceful lady and set up a school for young girls, even using her daughters as teachers. Mary began working there as soon as she entered her teens. From there, she attended a London school and was spotted by the actor David Garrick. Her mother was opposed to a career in the theatre for Mary, favouring the security of a husband who enjoyed a large inheritance. In the end, perhaps against her better judgement, Mary agreed and married Thomas Robinson. He had helped to look after her and her younger brother when both were ill, which persuaded her that he was a good man.

Unfortunately, he was also a liar. He had no inheritance nor much in the way of money at all and ended up in a debtor's prison just after their only child, a daughter named Mary Elizabeth, was born. It was while he was inside that Mary discovered the poetry she wrote for pleasure was popular. She published her first volume, 'Poems by Mrs Robinson' in 1775 and found a patron in the Duchess of Devonshire who helped her with her second volume, called 'Captivity'.

Realising that Thomas was never going to amount to much, even after his release, she set her mind on pursuing a career in the theatre that she probably should have followed all along. It was while she was performing as Perdita in 'A Winter's Tale' at Drury Lane that the Prince of Wales saw her and immediately fell in love. A situation to be repeated far too often in future years.

Mary withstood his advances for a long time; after all, a relationship with a prince would mean abandoning her acting career in which she was becoming increasingly successful. In the end, a promise of £20000 in compensation proved decisive. She agreed to become his mistress.

The relationship did not last too long. Within a couple of years, a message was despatched from the Prince of Wales confirming that he needed to end their now failing romance. In fact, he did not 'need' to do this, he just wanted to because another woman had taken his fancy. As far as the prince was concerned, that was that. He had moved on, so he could not fathom why Mary was upset by the decision. It was not just emotional loss (which was most likely limited in any case) that was causing her anguish. It was also the financial implications. She had given up her acting career and still had a child to support. Her husband was estranged and in any case, could offer little to his wife and child. Her thoughts turned to publishing once more, but this time, instead of poetry, she realised that the letters sent by the prince, blabbering with passion and intensity, would prove exceedingly popular and financially beneficial. News of her plans reached George III, who at this stage in his life was yet to suffer from the illness which would destroy him. Instead, he was still the frugal, careful but unsympathetic king of his earlier years. He was outraged and immediately awarded her £5000 in compensation for her agreement not to publish. It was not enough. The promised £20000 from Prince George had, unsurprisingly, not materialised. Now she produced his written guarantee of the sum. The household replied that the note was written when the prince was underage and, therefore, not binding. Like her mother before her, Mary was a resourceful woman. Now she offers to hand over the document in return for an annual annuity of £500, which would become £250 to her daughter in the event of her death.

The offer is accepted, and Mary's brief dalliance with royalty passes. She will go on to have other affairs, but in 1783 falls suddenly and becomes seriously ill. She recovers but is left partially paralysed. This is the trigger that sends her back to her writing, and she becomes prolific. She publishes eight novels, three plays, her memoirs and several more volumes of poetry. She becomes an advocate for women's rights and, maybe due to her unsatisfactory experiences with royalty, an arch advocate for the French Revolution.

But despite her allowance from the King and the small income from her books and other publications, money remains tight for Mary. She dies on Boxing Day 1800. She is only 44. Some fondness for the prince must remain as she requests that, on her death, a lock of her hair be sent to him. It is rumoured that this becomes another memento of his many affairs with which he shares his coffin.

Mary is the first of his numerous women with whom he enjoyed affairs. The last in this stream of mistresses is perhaps the one to whom the King, as he was by then, was closest. In fact, George IV became besotted with Elizabeth Conyngham, nee Denison (she was born in 1770), who gloried in the title of Marchioness Conyngham. For Elizabeth, though, it may have been that the relationship was more about social advancement and family name than actual love. Cynics might conclude that Elizabeth was a career mistress. Among her past conquests is no other than the Duke of Wellington. He claimed that it was her plan all along to win favour in the Regent's bedchamber, setting that as her goal in life from as far back as 1896, fourteen years before she achieved her aim.

As for the King, he took her as his mistress in 1820, just prior to his coronation. She was there at the Cathedral as he was crowned, reportedly he went as far as to wink and smile at her as she sat in the stalls. Although a Whig by persuasion, she recognised that the King held only minimal political sway and instead concentrated on using her position to promote her family and her husband. How strange must this seem to our modern ears? One's wife is the mistress of the King, and through that, one receives favours and positions. Certainly, that was the case for her husband, Henry Burton Conyngham, who was awarded the title of Marquess. Elizabeth's sons, too, were invested in the corridors of power. One becomes a Groom of the Bedchamber, a position as intimately close to the monarch as it is possible to be without actually sleeping with him; another is promoted to Master of the Robes.

Meanwhile, the infatuated King casts baubles aplenty at his romantic muse. Jewellery, use of homes in Windsor and at Brighton Pavilion, use of the King's horses and carriages. Gifts galore and expensive trinkets all find their way to her.

But every good thing comes to an end. On June 26th, 1830, the King died, and that marked the end of the Regency period, the good life of Elizabeth and the preferential treatment of her family. (Although her husband retains his position as Constable and Governor of Windsor Castle, which he keeps until his death two years later.) She must have been an unpopular figure in court because, by the next day, she is gone from the palace. Soon after, William IV expels her to Paris, where she lives until the new monarch dies, and the Victorian period begins. She returns then to the family estate in Kent, where she survives until the age of 92. Hardly a life of privations, but compared to that decade under the King's favour, a definite backwards step.

As for the King, what conclusions can be reached? The man who gave his name to the Regency period is a drunkard, a gambler, a man with no concept of commitment nor towards the sensibilities of others. He is entitled, arrogant and unpopular. He plays the soldier but never fights; he is constantly in debt and expects others to get him out of the fixes into which he thrusts himself.

Yet beneath the faults lie perhaps a couple of seams of goodness. He has a sensitivity to art; he mostly avoids politics recognising that it is a subject about which he knows little, and when he falls in love, it is genuine and heartfelt. At least most of the time, and admittedly not for long, but history suggests his passions are real. He is not without empathy, however hard he pushes the emotion to the bottom of his soul. He carries a lock of hair and a picture of a former lover with him to his grave. On his deathbed, the deathbed of the Regency period, he recognises that life has not been too bad overall, maybe even good. But that he could have made it a lot better.

CONCLUSION

LEGACIES OF THE REGENCY

What does the Regency leave behind for us? There are physical remains. The astonishing architecture from the likes of John Nash and his peers. The classical fashion – even the necktie, which has formed the basis of men's formal wear for centuries can trace its roots back to Regency and that pioneer of sartorial elegance, Beau Brummell. Then there is its cultural legacy, notably, of course, the great works of Austen and Mary Shelley, the poetry of the Romantics. They give us the inspiration for some of the most beautiful and entertaining stories of modern times – the productions of the likes of 'Pride and Prejudice' or even 'Bridgerton'. While the fashion for many art forms comes and goes, that of the Regency, its art, culture and fashion remain popular, and it is hard to imagine that this will ever change.

Because the Regency appeals to those weirdly linked fascinations, we hold for the romantic and beautiful, allied to the sordid and underhand. The excesses of the period were undoubtedly considerable but never so much so as to be considered depraved.

The Regency, or just before, gives us an independent America, with all the implications of that independence for the world… mostly good, occasionally bad.

But if those are the physical benefits (mostly) we take from the time, then the Regency leaves us with even greater, if less definable, legacies.

It is a time when social mobility raises its head. Not just in Britain but as the aristocracy across Europe is challenged, something must fill the void the gentry leaves behind. In Britain, change is much less dramatic, but the emergence of a widespread press, improving education, the abolition of the slave trade, and, essentially, the industrial revolution alters the existing order. The past will never completely return.

Perhaps most notably of all, the Regency is the point at which women begin their acceleration towards equality. They are humble and somewhat limited beginnings. Women live in a world dominated by men and misogyny. But it is a time when their talents and achievements can start to be recognised. They earn the right to choose who they will marry. Not an absolute right, it has to be said, and one governed by intricate levels of convention, but suddenly they can say 'No'. The arranged marriage, governed by advantage often for the husband but most frequently for the betrothed's family, dwindles and almost dies.

It is a time when women show they can be leaders in many fields historically associated with men: social change, science, astronomy, and engineering. The journey towards equality is still ongoing today.

But it was in the Regency period that women opened the door, stepped into the car and, for some of the time at least, sat behind the steering wheel.

Of course, mankind being what it is, there are lessons from the era that we did not take on board. Slavery is eventually banished, but racial discrimination remains a considerable issue across the world. Although – and maybe this is due to the Regency, at least in part – perhaps less so in the United Kingdom than in many places elsewhere.

Similarly, the rights of the LGBT+ are stronger in Britain than in a number of nations across the globe, but for all that, they are far from ideal. One wonders quite what Anne Lister or the Ladies of Llangollen would make of things if they could time travel forward to today. Life would be better and easier, no doubt, but still not perfect.

Industrialisation, too, has changed the world. It has brought about much good, many advances which make life better for the globe's population. And safer. Yet it is a concept the world embraced without considering the implications for the planet, cultural heritage and global conflict.

Still, we should not expect perfection. Travel to Brighton and marvel at the beautiful architecture, wander to the beach and see women dressed for comfort rather than in response to convention, get out your Jane Austen and enjoy.

The Regency gives us much of which we can be proud. And grateful.

REFERENCES

[1] Linning, S. (2022) The Real Bridgerton:…and let them die. The Mail Online. Retrieved from: The REAL Bridgerton: New book reveals the true scandals of the Regency period | Daily Mail Online

[2] BBC Elegance and Decadence the Age of the Regency Episode 1

[3] Turner, JMW. (1811) *Plymouth, from Mount Edgcumbe* (Painting)

[4] https://www.goodreads.com/quotes/8082-single-women-have-a-dreadful-propensity-for-being-poor-which-is

[5] British Library (ND) *Mirror of the GracesL Beauty and Fashion.* Retrieved from: The Mirror of the Graces: fashion and beauty manual | The British Library (bl.uk)

[6] Regency Culture and Society: On Female Politicians – Regency Reader (regrom.com)

[7] On Female Politicians – reprinted in the Lady's Monthly Museum, October 1800 edition

[8] Gilray, J. (1797) *The Gordon Knot – or – the bonny duchess hunting the Bedfordshire bull.* (Etching).Retrieved from: NPG D12610; 'The Gordon-knot, - or - the bonny-duchess hunting the Bedfordshire bull' - Portrait - National Portrait Gallery

[9] History Extra (2022). *Before Waterloo: What happened at the Duchess of Richmond's Ball?* Retrieved from: Belgravia: What Happened At The Duchess Of Richmond's Ball? | HistoryExtra

[10] Grantham Matters (2020). *Arbuthnot, Harriet – Best of friends with the Iron Duke* Retrieved from: Arbuthnot, Harriet – Best of friends with the Iron Duke (granthammatters.co.uk)

[11] Grantham Matters (2020). *Arbuthnot, Harriet – Best of friends with the Iron Duke* Retrieved from: Arbuthnot, Harriet – Best of friends with the Iron Duke (granthammatters.co.uk)

[12] Sarah Sophia Child-Villiers | NatWest Group Heritage Hub

[13] The News (London) Monday 14th November 1825 British Newspaper Archives

[14] Fanny Burney, British Novelist, Diarist, and Playwright, British Novelist, Diarist, and Playwright (literaryladiesguide.com)

[15] The News 1814 *Charlotte Dacre Obituary*. Retrieved from: The News. London: Monday, November J 4. | The News (London) | Monday 14 November 1825 | British Newspaper Archive

[16] The Jewish Lives Project (ND).*Charlotte Dacre*. Retrieved from: Charlotte Dacre | The Jewish Lives Project

[17] Rogers, S (1998) *Corvey 'Adopt an Author' – Elizabeth Ogilvy Benger*. Retrieved from: Corvey | Adopt an Author (shu.ac.uk)

[18] Escarpit, R. (1998) *Germaine de Stael*. Retrieved from: Germaine de Staël | French-Swiss author | Britannica

[19] Marshall,F. Marshall, J. Shelley, M. (1889) *The Life and Letters of Mary Wollstonecraft Shelley. London. Richard Bentley and Son*

[20] JaneAusten.org. (ND) *Jane Austen Biography*. Retrieved from: Jane Austen Biography

[21] Welsh Icons News. (ND) *Sarah Siddons*. Retrieved from: Welsh Icons News | Sarah Siddons

[22] Hayne, J (1824) *Mr Hayne and Miss Foote.* Morning Post. Page 3. Retrieved from: Mr. Hayne and Miss Foote. | Morning Post | Saturday 16 October 1824 | British Newspaper Archive

[23] Lathan, S. (2017) *Three Famed Regency Actresses: Siddons, Davison, Kemble.* Retrieved from: Three Famed Regency Actresses: Siddons, Davison, Kemble - Sharon Lathan, Novelist (sharonlathanauthor.com)

[24] HLB, Intriguing History. (2016). *Sarah Guppy an English Inventor.* Retrieved from: Sarah Guppy an English inventor (intriguing-history.com)

[25] Caroline Herschel." Famous Scientists. famousscientists.org. 3 Apr. 2018. Web. 6/29/2022 <www.famousscientists.org/caroline-herschel/>

[26] English Heritage. (ND) *Women in History – Dido Elizabeth Belle.* Retrieved from: Dido Belle | English Heritage (english-heritage.org.uk)

[27] Jay, M. (2022). *Edward and Catherine Despard.* Retrieved from: Edward and Catherine Despard - Mike Jay

[28] Dalrymple, W. (ND) *Love and Betrayalin India: The White Mughal.* Retrieved from: BBC Four - Love and Betrayal in India: The White Mughal - A love story that broke the conventional boundaries of Empire

[29] Mitchell, M. (2022) *Who Sings the Gentleman Jack Song? Origins behind the theme tune.* Retrieved from: Who Sings the 'Gentleman Jack' Song? Origins Behind the Theme Tune (newsweek.com)

[30] Woods, R. (2019) *The Life and Loves of Anne Lister.* Retrieved from: The Life and Loves of Anne Lister - BBC News

[31] The Morning Advertiser (24/1/1833). *Yesterday evening, at half past eight o clock...* Retrieved from: £s\ €' ■7" Yesterday Evening, At Half-Past Eight O'clock, Inqnisltion Was Held Before Mr. Higgs, At The Coach Mad Hones, | Morning Advertiser | Thursday 24 January 1833 | British Newspaper Archive

[32] Eleanor Butler 1739-1829, Sarah Ponsonby 1755-1831

[33] Lady Caroline Lamb Facts & Information - Lord Byron's Lovers (englishhistory.net) Hanson, Marilee. "Lady Caroline Lamb Facts & Information – Lord Byron's Lovers" <a href="https://englishhistory.net/byron/lady-caroline-lamb/">https://englishhistory.net/byron/lady-caroline-lamb/</a>, February 1, 2015

[34] Lady Caroline Lamb Facts & Information - Lord Byron's Lovers (englishhistory.net) Hanson, Marilee. "Lady Caroline Lamb Facts & Information – Lord Byron's Lovers" <a href="https://englishhistory.net/byron/lady-caroline-lamb/">https://englishhistory.net/byron/lady-caroline-lamb/</a>, February 1, 2015

[35] Macoherson, H. (2019). *The story of Grace Elliot's incredible life – from high society to spy to author.* Retrieved from: The story of Grace Elliot's incredible life – from high society to spy to author | The National

Thank you for reading my book.

I hope you enjoyed reading **Real Women Of The Regency** and have gained a deeper appreciation for these women.

If you liked the book I would be grateful if you left a review on Amazon Review. It is really important as a self-publisher to get reviews.

Point your phone camera at the QR codes to leave a review on Amazon.

Printed in Great Britain
by Amazon

16903562R00124